Splendor of Tibet
The Potala Palace

Edited by Phuntsok Namgyal

Photographs by

Staff at Encyclopedia of China Publishing House

Homa & Sekey Books

in association with

Encyclopedia of China Publishing House

FIRST AMERICAN EDITION

ISBN: 1-931907-02-1
Library of Congress Control Number: 2002102109

Publishers Cataloging-in-Publication Data

Splendor of Tibet: The Potala Palace
Edited by Phuntsok Namgyal

1. Potala (Lhasa, China) — Pictorial works — History
2. Tibet (China) — travel
3. Painting and architecture — China — Lhasa
4. Buddhism — Tibetan

I. Title   DS796.L46 2002   951/.5-dc21

Published by Homa & Sekey Books
138 Veterans Plaza
P. O. Box 103
Dumont, NJ 07628
U.S.A

Tel: (201)384-6692
Fax: (201)384-6055
Email: info@homabooks.com
Website: www.homabooks.com

Editor: Shawn X. Ye

Published by arrangement with
Encyclopedia of China Publishing House
17 Fuchengmen Bei Dajie
Beijing, 100037
China

Printed in China

contents

The world-famous Potala Palace stands on the Red Hill overlooking the city of Lhasa in Tibet.

At an elevation of more than 12,000 feet (3,700 meters) above the sea level, the Potala is the world's highest and largest castle palace. Built against the terraced slope of the hill, with buildings one upon another, the Potala has an imposing look. The granite walls, the reddish-brown walls made of willow branches, golden roofs decorated with big gilded bottles, the splendid sutra-streamers and banners are unique characteristics of the Potala buildings. The striking contrast of red, white and yellow colors join to make the Potala a rare example of architecture in the traditional Tibetan style.

The structure is composed of the White Palace and the Red Palace. The 7-story White Palace served as the winter residence of successive Dalai Lamas. It also housed the former local Tibetan government. On its fourth floor is the Eastern Audience Hall, the biggest in the White Palace, where important political and religious ceremonies such as the enthronement of Dalai Lamas were held. On the top of the

The Potala Palace
A Brief Introduction

palace are two apartments of Dalai Lamas' winter residence, known as the East and West Sunshine Apartments.

The Red Palace consists primarily of Dalai Lamas' stupa halls and various chapels. It contains eight Dalai Lamas stupas and chapels, including the West Audience Hall, Dharmaraja Cave and the Chapel Celebrating Victory over the Three Worlds. The West Audience Hall, the Fifth Dalai Lama's memorial hall, is the largest hall in the entire Potala complex. The Dharmaraja Cave and some other sections, which can be dated back to the Tubo regime in the seventh century, are among the earliest buildings of the Potala. While the Chapel Celebrating Victory over the Three Worlds is the highest hall in the Red Palace, the hall housing the Thirteenth Dalai Lama's stupa is the latest building of the Potala.

Subordinate constructions to the Potala include the Namgyel Dratsang, the training center for monk officials, the monks' dormitories, and the eastern and western courtyards on the hill, the printing house for Buddhist scriptures, a jail, stables and the Dragon King's Pool at the backyard of the Potala at the foot of the hill.

The initiator of the Potala can be traced back to Tubo Tsenpo Songtsen Gampo, a Tibetan king, who began to build the Potala in 631 (the Iron-Hare year by the Tibetan calendar). The Potala at that time had 999 rooms, with the addition of a cave shrine, making the figure up to 1,000. Later, due to fires caused by lightning and wars, the original construction was almost leveled to the ground. Construction of the present Potala began in 1645 in the reign of the Fifth Dalai Lama, who, in order to consolidate the Ganden Potrang political-religious regime, rebuilt the White Palace as well as the enclosures, towers and turrets of the Potala. He subsequently moved his government to the White Palace from the Drepung

Monastery. In 1690, the Sixth Dalai Lama enlarged the Red Palace to house the Fifth Dalai Lama's stupa. The extension was completed in 1693, which was followed by new projects, including five golden roofs and a number of subordinate sections, sponsored by later Dalai Lamas. By 1936, when the Thirteenth Dalai Lama's stupa was built, the Potala we see today was completed.

Over the past 300 years or so, the Potala has accumulated an enormous collection of historical relics, including a great number of murals, about 1,000 pagodas, 10,000 statues, numerous Tangka paintings, Buddhist scriptures, and gold and silver objects.

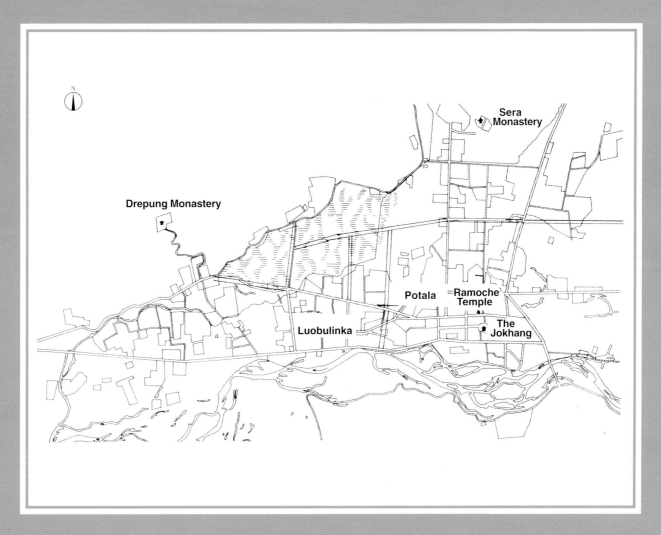

The location of the Potala Palace in Lhasa

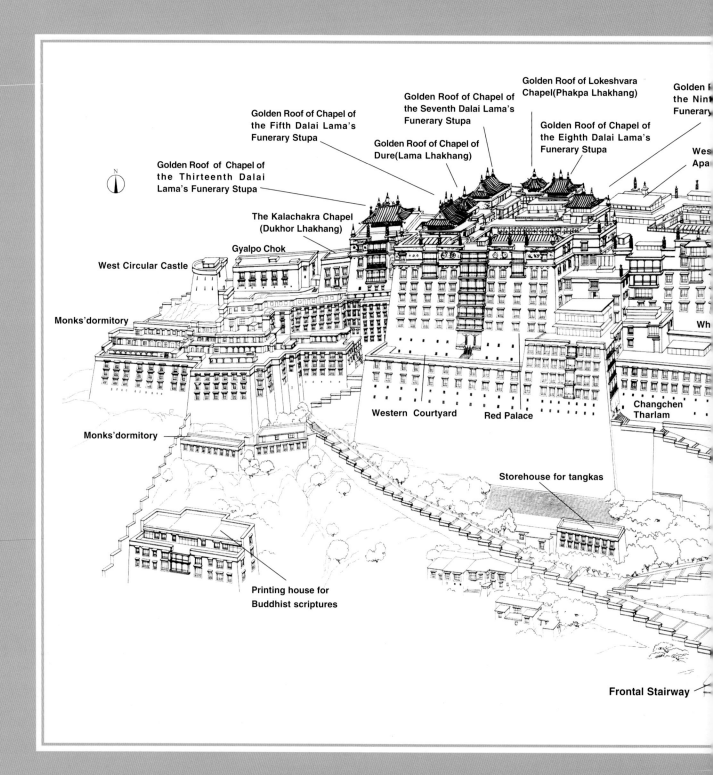

Golden Roof of Lokeshvara Chapel(Phakpa Lhakhang)

Golden Roof of Chapel of the Seventh Dalai Lama's Funerary Stupa

Golden Roof of Chapel of the Fifth Dalai Lama's Funerary Stupa

Golden Roof of Chapel of Dure(Lama Lhakhang)

Golden Roof of Chapel of the Eighth Dalai Lama's Funerary Stupa

Golden R the Nin Funerary

Golden Roof of Chapel of the Thirteenth Dalai Lama's Funerary Stupa

Wes Apa

The Kalachakra Chapel (Dukhor Lhakhang)

Gyalpo Chok

West Circular Castle

Monks' dormitory

Wh

Monks' dormitory

Western Courtyard

Red Palace

Changchen Tharlam

Storehouse for tangkas

Printing house for Buddhist scriptures

Frontal Stairway

A Bird's-eye view of the Potala Palace

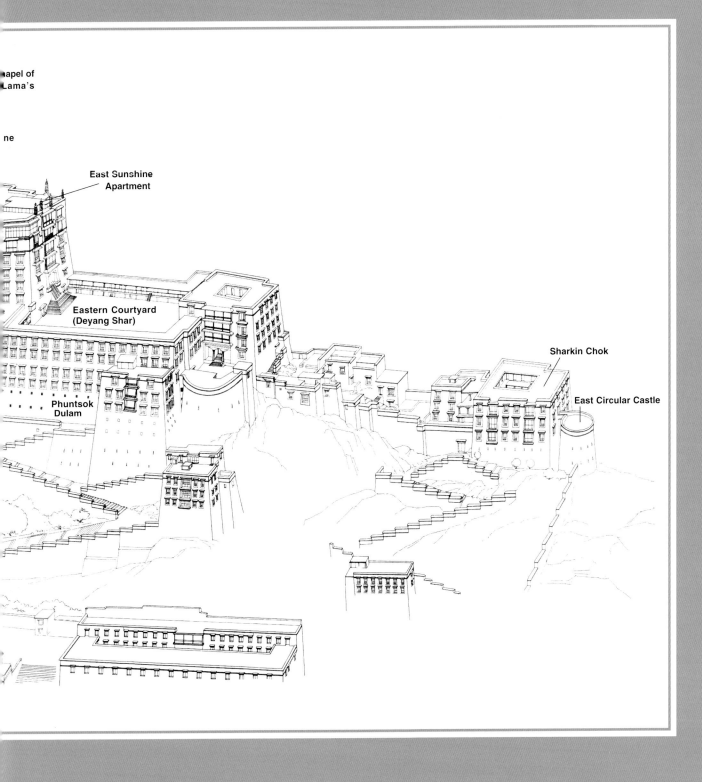

apel of
Lama's

ne

East Sunshine
Apartment

Eastern Courtyard
(Deyang Shar)

Sharkin Chok

East Circular Castle

Phuntsok
Dulam

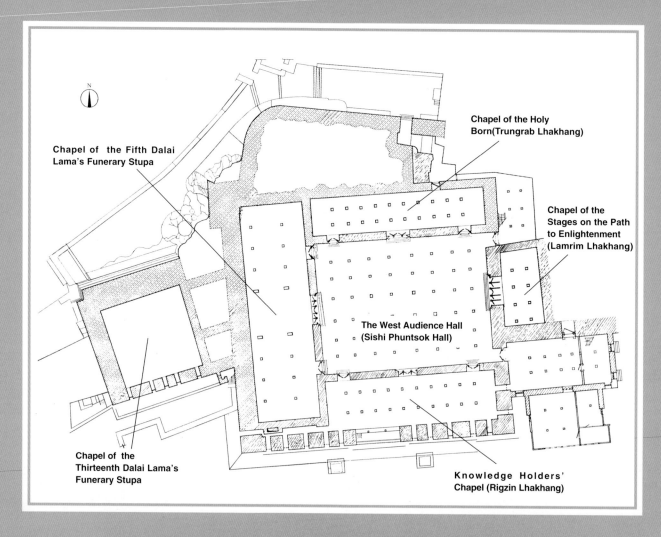

Chapel of the Fifth Dalai
Lama's Funerary Stupa

Chapel of the Holy
Born(Trungrab Lhakhang)

Chapel of the
Stages on the Path
to Enlightenment
(Lamrim Lhakhang)

The West Audience Hall
(Sishi Phuntsok Hall)

Chapel of the
Thirteenth Dalai Lama's
Funerary Stupa

Knowledge Holders'
Chapel (Rigzin Lhakhang)

Chapels and Halls on the first floor of the Red Palace

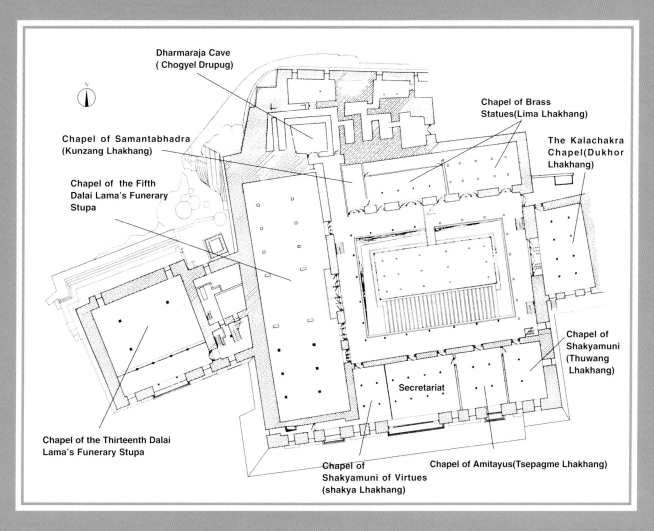

Dharmaraja Cave
(Chogyel Drupug)

Chapel of Brass
Statues(Lima Lhakhang)

Chapel of Samantabhadra
(Kunzang Lhakhang)

The Kalachakra
Chapel(Dukhor
Lhakhang)

Chapel of the Fifth
Dalai Lama's Funerary
Stupa

Chapel of
Shakyamuni
(Thuwang
Lhakhang)

Secretariat

Chapel of the Thirteenth Dalai
Lama's Funerary Stupa

Chapel of
Shakyamuni of Virtues
(shakya Lhakhang)

Chapel of Amitayus(Tsepagme Lhakhang)

Chapels and Halls on the third floor of the Red Palace

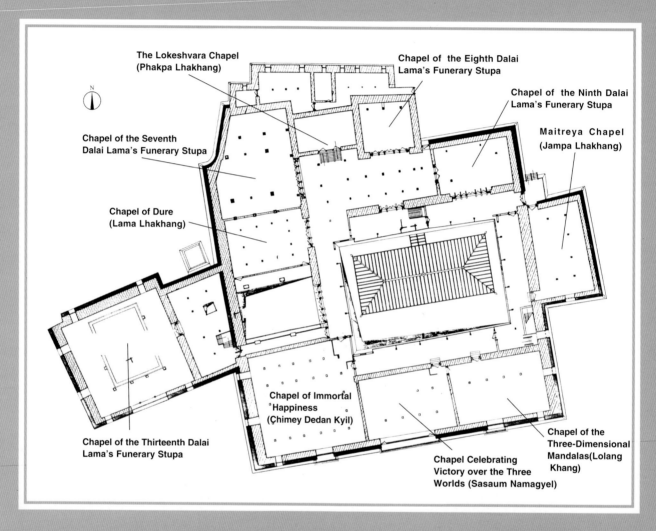

The Lokeshvara Chapel
(Phakpa Lhakhang)

Chapel of the Eighth Dalai
Lama's Funerary Stupa

Chapel of the Ninth Dalai
Lama's Funerary Stupa

Maitreya Chapel
(Jampa Lhakhang)

Chapel of the Seventh
Dalai Lama's Funerary Stupa

Chapel of Dure
(Lama Lhakhang)

Chapel of Immortal
Happiness
(Chimey Dedan Kyil)

Chapel of the
Three-Dimensional
Mandalas(Lolang
Khang)

Chapel of the Thirteenth Dalai
Lama's Funerary Stupa

Chapel Celebrating
Victory over the Three
Worlds (Sasaum Namagyel)

Chapels and Halls on the fourth floor of the Red Palace

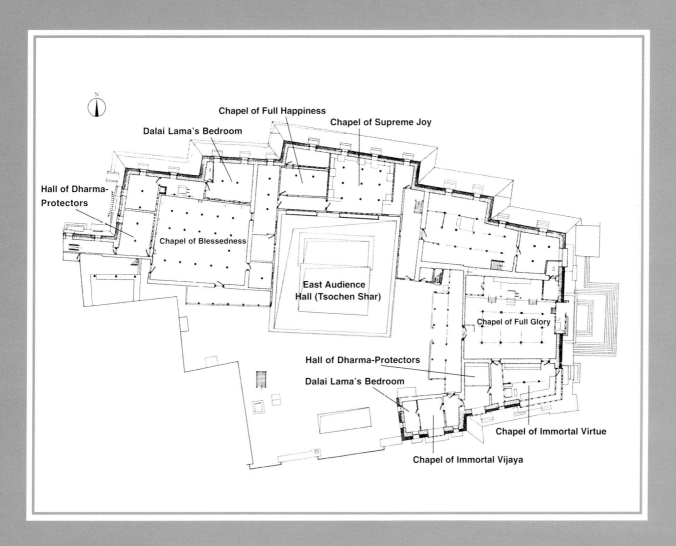

Chapels and Halls on the Sunshine Apartment
on the top floor of the White Palace

An Overall View of the Potala

The Potala stands against the terraced slope of the Red Hill. Its main portion is a building of 13 stories. The major parts of the Potala include the Red Palace, the White Palace, and monks' dormitories. In addition, there are the old town Zhol and the Dragon King's Pool at the foot of the hill. In 1961, the State Council placed the Potala on the list of cultural sites under State-level protection. In 1994 the UNESCO World Heritage Committee placed the Potala on the World Cultural Heritage list.

The Potala

The name "Potala" is a derivation from Sanskrit Potaraka, meaning "Brilliant Mountain," "Island Mountain," or "Boat Mountain," which is dedicated to Avalokiteshvara. Qing Emperor Kangxi said in a stele installed on Mt. Putuo of Zhejiang, "As recorded in Buddhist scriptures, there are three Potaraka mountains: one is at a port of the Indus, another is in Tibet, and the third is the sacred island of Putuo in the South Sea."

The Potala is the best palace complex of Tibet well-kept till now. It is a landmark of Tibet well-known to the world, and it is a very important cultural relic site under State-level protection of China. It was listed as an important world historical heritage by UNESCO in December, 1994.

Buddhist Pagodas on the Square of the Potala (Trakor Karnyi)

The three pagodas on the western side of the Potala Square are called Trakor Karnyi in Tibetan. The legend says that the pagodas were built by Princess Jincheng, who was the Tang Emperor Zhongzong's stepdaughter and married to the then Tubo King. Of the three pagodas, the one in the middle is called Miraculous Pagoda and it is the highest. To its north is Victorious Pagoda, located at the foot of the Red Hill. The Bodhi Pagoda is to the south of the Miraculous Pagoda, located at the foot of Chakpori.

► The Non-inscribed Stone Stele (Dokri Langma)

The stone stele without any words inscribed on it was erected in 1693 for the inauguration of the Fifth Dalai Lama's funerary stupa. The stele stands at the bottom of the southern stone stairway that leads to the Potala. It is over 18 feet high. Its top part, body, and bottom are made of granite. The Fifth Dalai Lama died in 1682. Because of political and religious reasons his death was not reported to the Qing government for 13 years. The Fifth Dalai Lama's funerary stupa and the hall to house it began to be built in 1690. When the Fifth Dalai Lama's funerary stupa was completed in 1693, a stele without any words on it was erected in commemoration of the occasion.

The Frontal Stairway ◄

The front stairway of the Potala is about 1,000 feet long and 16-25 feet wide. From the Non-inscribed Stone Stele the stairway leads westward to the upper and lower dormitories of monks; and eastward to the entrance of Red Palace, through the Monk Official Training School to the eastern courtyard of the White Palace, and to the Victory Castle.

Reddish-Brown Walls Made of Willow Branches and Copper Lions ▶

The building complex of the Red Palace is in four colors: red walls, black window frames, white window eaves, and reddish-brown walls made of willow branches. Each of the four roof-corners has a gilded copper statue of lion, three feet high. In Buddhist canon the Buddha is regarded as a lion. So the seat of a statue of Buddha or Bodhisattva and that for an eminent monk when he preaches Buddhism is called the "Lion Seat." Lion becomes one of the important themes of monastery construction.

Great Enlightenment Entrance

The Great Enlightenment Entrance is the name of the main gate to the Red Palace. Four pillars stand in the ante-hall. The pillars and beams are carved with beautiful patterns, "Eight Auspicious Symbols," pictures of Buddha, and those of auspicious animals such as lion, peacock, deer, and kylin, etc. The name of the entrance is inscribed on a rectangular tablet at the door lintel.

The Back Stairway

The Potala can be reached by a way from the western gate of the Red Hill through the Horse Route to the Wangkhang building of the Red Palace. It was built specially for the Dalai Lama and high officials of the Kashag (former local Tibetan government) to go to the Potala on horseback or by sedan-chairs. Carts can also run on it.

Lake of the Naga-king (Lukhang)

Located at the back, or the northern side, of the Potala, the lake was formed from a big hole from which a large amount of earth was taken for the reconstruction of the Potala in the second half of the 17th century. It is said that the Sixth Dalai Lama moved the Naga-king of Medrogunkar in the eastern suburbs of Lhasa to the pool, and thus it was called the Lake of the Naga King. In 1791, the Eighth Dalai Lama Jampel Gyatso repaired and maintained the building on the lake. It is said that the Protector Deity and Precious-Vase Mandala that Princess Wencheng brought to Tibet are enshrined in the Naga Chapel on the isle in the lake.

The Back Gate ◄

The back gate (western gate) is in the southwest corner at the foot of the Red Hill. The gate leads to the back side of the Potala. The gate did not appear in the photo of the Potala in 1905. It was only after 1952 that the gate and enclosure were built for safeguarding the Potala.

21

The Eastern Courtyard (Deyang Shar)

It is a broad terrace in front of the entrance to the White Palace. It is flanked from west by the main building of the White Palace and from east by the Training Center for Monk Officials, while dormitories line it from north and south. On the 22nd through the 29th day of the 12th month by Tibetan calendar, masked lamas would perform at the Eastern Courtyard religious dances for driving ghosts.

The Eastern Courtyard (Deyang Shar)

The picture shows the high-rising building of the White Palace and its eastern courtyard. The courtyard, with an area of about 2,400 square yards, is the largest in the Potala. To its south and north are corridors and dormitories, to the east is the Monk Officials Training School, and to the west are staircases. A Buddhist meeting for worshiping the Buddha is held here each year on the 29th day of the 12th month of Tibetan calendar. This is a religious dancing ritual symbolizing the old year passing off. The Dalai Lama usually watched from the East Sunhine Apartment the religious dance performed by Namgyel Dratsang's monks.

The Antechamber to the White Palace

Richly decorated with murals, it leads to the entrance to the White Palace. The Four Guardian Kings of the East, the West, the South, and the North (Dhritarashtra, Virupaksha, Virudhaka, and Vaishravana) appear on its south, north, and west walls. On the south wall are an illustration of Vinaya and sutra, a picture of three monks protecting the Dharma, and the edicts and handwriting of the Fifth Dalai Lama. On the eastern wall are pictures of the Jokhang Temple, the Barkor, the Potala in the 7th century, the five tests given to the Tibetan envoy by the Tang emperor, and the picture of Princess Wencheng's journey to Tibet. At both sides of the staircase are the pictures of verses that can be read either backward or forward.

The Main Gate to the White Palace

The Main Gate to the White Palace consists of two planks with carved decorations and a hemispheric ring. The doorframes are decorated with various patterns of grass and flower. The lintel is gilded and beautifully painted.

The antechamber to the White Palace (Kalpo) ►

The antechamber is on the 4th floor of the main building of the White Palace. East of it is an octagonal door-hole without frame and plank, so that the antechamber is full of sunlight. The antechamber has four pillars, each three feet in diameter and ten feet high. With exquisite carving and murals the antechamber is the most magnificent part of the White Palace.

Beautifully Carved Beams and Pillars

The picture shows the beautifully carved pillars and beams in the antechamber of the White Palace. Each part of the pillars is tightly connected with the other. There are patterns of the Buddha, Sanskrit letters, lotus-flower, tassel, grass, Dharma-wheel, and animals on the pillars and beams. The beams are painted in red as basic color, on which are paintings in blue, green, and gold. This is a characteristic feature of colored carving and painting on Tibetan construction.

"Princess Wencheng's Journey to Tibet" and Other Murals ◄

The mural is on the east side of the northern wall in the antechamber to the White Palace. In the upper part is the scene of Princess Wencheng's journey to Tibet in the mid-7th century, the Buddha statue (now the main image worshipped in the Jokhang Temple) she brought to Tibet being carried by a cart, and the welcome ceremony held for her. In the lower part is the scene of the Jokhang Temple starting to be built: Princess Wencheng making divination for choosing a site of the temple, goats carrying earth to fill the lake, and the construction being completed by Princess Trisun.

Murals of Verses That Can Be Read Backward or Forward and Still Make Sense ►

The two murals are at the top of the stairway leading to the eastern entrance to the White Palace. They are 2.2 feet high and 2.6 feet wide. The verse on the north is in square form with the Six-Words Dharani of Om-Mani-Padme-Hum of Tibetan Buddhism as its content, and on the south is that in circular form with a poem written by Tsongkhapa as its content.

The East Audience Hall (Tsochen Shar)

With 34 pillars, it is the main and the largest hall in the White Palace. At the north is the Dalai Lama's throne, over which hangs a tablet inscribed with Chinese characters "Promoter of the Faith and Defender of Frontier Peace," written by the Qing Emperor Tongzhi. On the four walls inside the hall there are various murals. There are pictures of the founder of the Geluk order, Tsongkhapa with his two chief disciples, and Six Ornaments and Two Supreme Buddhist philosophers of ancient India. An illustration of the groundwork of the Samye Monastery, and the First, Second, Third, and Fourth Dalai Lamas' portraits are on the south wall. Drom Tonpa and some saints' portraits are on the west. The portraits of Chogyel Drakpa, Trisong Detsen, the Fifth Dalai Lama, Songtsen Gampo, Tritsug Detsen, and Shakyamuni, and a picture of Ramoche Temple are on the northern wall. The murals on the northern wall are the reappearance of the first phase of maintenance of the Potala during 1989–1994, a project of high research value. Important ceremonies such as the Dalai Lamas' enthronement were held here.

The Mural of the Portrait of the First Dalai Lama

The mural is in the center of the south side of the East Audience Hall of the White Palace. The image is the First Dalai Lama Gendun Drupa (1391-1474), kind and dignified in appearance. He wears the robes of a monk and a yellow hat. His right arm is bare and his right hand makes a gesture of generosity. His left hand holds a lotus flower. He sits on a lotus throne, cross-legged in Vajra posture, with a Dharma-wheel in front, and a halo behind.

Mural: Delivering a Sermon

The mural is on the east wall of the Eastern Audience Hall in the White Palace. It depicts a Buddhist master preaching Buddhism before monks in the reign of Tubo Tsenpo Trisong Detsen, when the territory was wide, the people lived in peace, and Buddhism was prosperous.

Mural

The mural is on the east wall of the East Audience Hall in the White Palace. It shows a joyful scene of the people living in peace during the reign of Trisong Detsen. Trisong Detsen (reigned 755-797) reigned for more than forty years, during the period owing to his civil and military achievements, Tubo's territory was expanded to Huihe in the north, Tazig (Persia) in the west, Hindu in the south, and Nanzhao in the east. Tubo was at the top of its prosperity. He supported Buddhism, was the first Tsenpo who allowed Tibetans to become monks, and sponsored the construction of the Samye Monastery, which began in 765, and completed 12 years later. He was regarded as one of the three religious kings of Tibet (Songtsen Gampo, Trisong Detsen, and Tritsug Detsen).

The West Sunshine Apartment

Located at the western part of the top floor of the White Palace, it served as the Dalai Lamas' living chambers and offices. Its name suggests that the apartment is full of sunshine. It consists of the Chapel of Blessedness, Chapel of Full Happiness, Chapel of Supreme Joy, the Hall of Dharma-protectors, and bedrooms.

Chapel of Full Happiness (Phuntsok Topgye)

It is to the northeast of the Full-Blessedness Chapel of West Sunshine Apartment in the White Palace of the Potala, and to the west of the Supreme Joy Chapel. The West Sunshine Apartment is Dalai Lama's bedroom, and it was built in 1645. Owing to the fact that it is at the top of the White Palace and is fully exposed to sunlight, the bedroom is bathed in brilliant sunshine all the day. Hence it is called Sunshine Apartment.

Mural

The mural is on the northern wall of the Chapel of Blessedness in the West Sunshine Apartment of the White Palace. It is a story of "protecting wealth" in the 29th chapter of *Good-luck Precious Cane*, a book about the life of the Buddha.

Mural

The mural is on the northern wall of the Chapel of Blessedness in the West Sunshine Apartment of the White Palace. It is six feet high and is about the story of "the meeting of father and son," described in the 20th chapter of *Avadana-shataka (Wish-Fulfilling Precious Cane)*, a book of 108 chapters about the life of Shakyamuni written by Gewep of ancient India. The *Wish-Fulfilling Precious Cane* is collected in the Tengyur of Tibetan Tripitaka.

► **Mural**

The mural is on the northern wall of the Chapel of Blessedness in the West Sunshine Apartment of the White Palace, six feet high. It is a story about the Buddha's descent from Sumeru, i.e. a Jataka story.

34

The Chapel of Supreme Joy (Ganden Yangtse)

It is located to the east of the Chapel of Full Happiness. It has nine pillars, of which the middle one is the longest and reaches the ceiling. A throne of the Dalai Lama is at the north wall. Along the walls are Buddhist shrines. In the shrines are beautifully shaped small images of Buddha, most of which are offerings. The Thirteenth Dalai Lama used to live in the West Sunshine Apartment.

► **Niches**

The niches are on the east side of the Supreme Joy Chapel in the White Palace. Buddhism consists of Mahayana and Hinayana, and there are exoteric and esoteric sects. Different sects worship different Buddhas or deities. The niches on the east side of the Supreme Joy Chapel house images of Nechung oracle, Pelden Lhamo, and White Tara. The niches on the northern side house those of Pelden Lhamo, Yamantaka, Yama, Tsongkhapa and the Fifth Dalai Lama, and those in the western side include that of Protector deity Tsemare.

The East Sunshine Apartment

Located in the east part of the top floor of the White Palace, it was enlarged and served as the Thirteenth Dalai Lama's residence in his old age. It consists of the Chapel of Full Glory, Chapel of Immortal Virtue, Hall of Protector Deity, Chapel of Immortal Vijaya, and bedrooms. The Tsekhang at the entrance to the Chapel of Full Glory was an administration office in charge of receiving guests, delivering Dalai Lama's decrees and transmit orders of appointing and removing lay and monk officials. The chief of the Tsekhang was Dronyer, who had the right to report to the Dalai Lama the local government officials' behavior.

The Chapel of Full Glory (Ganden Namsel)

This chapel is the largest sutra-chanting hall in the East Sunshine Apartment. It is square in the floor plan, faces south and has 12 pillars. There are big windows on the four sides under the ceiling. In the north a throne of Dalai Lama is on a platform which is flanked by the Dalai Lama's study room and toilet. On the eastern side by the window is the place for the Dalai Lama to watch opera performance, and the southern side leads to the Chapel of Immortal Virtue, the Hall of Protector Deity, and the Dalai's bedroom.

Tangkas

Tangka is a popular religious scroll painting in Tibetan areas. The painting is usually made on cotton or silk. The scroll painting is easy to carry about, so it is used by Tibetan people in their daily life. There are paper, cotton, and silk tangkas; and there are tangkas of silk polychrome, silk embroidery, and tapestry. It has a very wide range of subject matter, including stories about Buddha, images of Buddha and bodhisattvas, Gurus, patriarchs, and Protectors, biography, history, science, technology, and folklore. It can be said that the tangkas are an encyclopaedia of Tibetan culture. This tangka is on the wall of the East Sunshine Apartment. It is one in a series of the tangkas about the Six Ornaments and Two Supreme Buddhist philosophers of India.

Mural about Shambhala

The mural is in the center of the western wall of the Full Glory Chapel in the East Sunshine Apartment of the White Palace. It is about two feet in diameter. According to Records of Tibetan Kings and Ministers, when Chandrabhava, the first king of Shambhala kingdom, brought the Kalachakra-Vajra Sutra back to his country, stopped halfway in the great forest of Malaya and built the Mandala of Perfection there. Since then all living beings in Shambhala share Vajra Vehicle and thirty-three kings one after another ascended the Fearless-lion Throne. The mandala in the mural shows Shambhala as an ideal place surrounded by snow-capped mountains in the form of eight lotus petals with rivers flowing among them, and Kalachakra Sutra spreading everywhere.

Mural: Shakyamuni's miraculous transformations

The mural is in the center of the southern wall of the Full Glory Chapel, which is in the East Sunshine Apartment of the White Palace. The mural depicts the Buddha's various miraculous transformations in subduing evil spirits and demons.

The Chapel of Immortal Virtue (Takten Palshe)

The chapel is in the southeast corner of the East Sunshine Apartment in the White Palace. Its floor plan is in the ladder-shaped form. It is Dalai Lama's private chapel and audience room. In the room are exquisite niches and a chair of the Dalai Lama's. With a big window in the southeast corner, the room is bathed in sunshine. It has a passageway leading to the Chapel of Full Glory. The ceiling is covered with silk and satin curtains.

► Tangka of Gurus

The tangka hangs over the seat of the Dalai Lama in the Chapel of Immortal Virtue in the East Sunshine Apartment of the White Palace. It is made on a piece of cotton. It shows a group of Gurus sitting in the form of a "Wish-fulfilling Tree." There are a total of 357 images of Tibetan Buddhist Gelukpa masters on the tree.

42

The Hall of Protector Deity

The hall is by the side of the Chapel of Immortal Virtue in the East Sunshine Apartment. From here one can go to the west antechamber. The floor plan of the hall is rectangular. The shrines there house the images of Nechung Protector, Kapala Protector, Six-armed Guhyasamaja, and Pelden Lhamo. Dalai Lama often practiced meditation in the hall.

► Tangka of Tsongkhapa

This tangka of Tsongkhapa hangs right over the throne of the Dalai Lama in the Protector Deity Hall of the East Sunshine Apartment in the White Palace. It is made on a piece of cotton. In its center is the image of Tsongkhapa, founder of the Geluk order of Tibetan Buddhism. He wears the robes of a monk and a yellow hat. His hands are held to his heart in the gesture of teaching, or "turning the wheel of Dharma." He sits cross-legged on a lotus throne, with his two chief disciples, Gyeltsab Je and Khedrup Je, standing by.

Mural: Yamantaka (or Vajrabhairava)

The tangka of Yamantaka is by the side of that of Tsongkhapa over the throne of the Dalai Lama in the Protector Deity Hall of the East Sunshine Apartment of the White Palace. It is made on a piece of cotton. In its center is an image of Yamantaka (or Vajrabhairava); he is a special protector of the Tibetan Esoteric Buddhism. According to Esoteric Buddhism, Vajrabhairava means the "Destroyer of Death." He is a wrathful manifestation of Manjushri.

► Tangka of Eleven-Headed Avalokiteshvara

The tangka is in the west end of the Protector Deity Hall of the East Sunshine Apartment in the White Palace. The eleven-faced and Thousand-armed Avalokiteshvara is a savior of Tibetan Buddhism. He has four rows of four heads. The head on the top represents that of Amitayus. He has eight main hands, the middle two of which hold together; those on the right side hold rosary, and make the gesture of fearlessness and the gesture of turning the dharma-wheel; and those on the left hold lotus flower, vase, bow and arrow, making the gesture of wish-fulfilling. The thousand arms, each with an eye spreading to all sides, look like a halo at his back.

47

The Chapel of Immortal Vijaya (Chimey Namgyel)

The chapel is located to the east of Dalai Lama's bedroom in the East Sunshine Apartment of the White Palace. It communicates with the bedroom and passageway. Thus the chapel is bathed in brilliant sunshine. It was a place for Dalai Lama's daily activities.

Statue of Manjushri

This statue of Manjushri is in the East Sunshine Apartment. Manjushri, the bodhisattva of wisdom, is shown as a beautiful youth with a golden yellow complexion. Manjushri is an embodiment of the discriminative awareness (prajna) of all the Buddhas (the fully enlightened mind). He is normally depicted as holding a sword in his right hand and a scripture in his left hand. In Buddhist iconography one finds various aspects of Manjushri, some with multiple faces and arms. Manjushri is also the name of an eminent historical figure, who was one of the eight principal bodhisattva disciples of the Buddha.

The Maitreya Chapel (Jampa Lhakhang)

The main image here is a gilded copper statue of Maitreya. To its right is a silver statue of White Tara, and statues of Amitayus and Vijaya, and to its left are gilded copper statues of Kshitigarbha, goddess Dondrup Drolma, and Acala. The throne of the Eighth Dalai Lama is on the west side. Originally this chapel was the "Ganden Phuntsok Hall" of the Eighth Dalai Lama, but it was renamed as Maitreya Chapel in 1800.

A Part of the Chapel of Maitreya

The main statue Maitreya here is in the middle of the east side of the chapel, which is flanked by Kshitigarbha, Dondup Drolma, Acala, White Tara, Amitayus, and Vijaya. In the middle of the west side is the throne of the Eighth Dalai Lama Jampel Gyatso. There are also the statues of Kalachakra, Atisha, Tsongkhapa, and Songtsen Gampo. The shrines along the walls house the statues of Tsongkhapa, the Fifth Dalai Lama, and Kangyur, etc.

Statue of Maitreya (Jampa)

In the middle of the east side of the Maitreya Chapel is a gilded copper statue of Maitreya, about 12 feet high and 9 feet wide. Maitreya wears a five-petal crown and big earrings. Smiling, he holds a dharma-wheel in the right hand and a vase in the left hand. Wearing a silk robe of bodhisattva, he is seated on a throne, facing west. The background behind him is a big halo with the patterns of "Six Sacred Beings." According to Buddhist canon, Maitreya was born in a Brahman family in the south of India. He became a disciple of the Buddha. Afterwards he ascended to Tushita, but in 5 billion and 670 million years would descend on the world again. He is regarded as the next Buddha after Shakyamuni.

Golden Roofs

The Potala has seven golden roofs, referring to the gilded roofs of the stupa chapels and the main hall. Among the gilded decoration objects on the roofs are bell or bottle styled "precious bottles," whose lotus-throne, the wheel on the throne, the bell on the wheel, the bottle on the bell, and the pearl on the top are said to represent Amitayus, Amitabha, Amoghasiddhi, Acala, and Ratnasambhava respectively. Around the roofs are hung various religious banners and sutra-streamers.

Golden Roofs

The golden roofs refer to the roofs of the Red Palace in the Potala. There are seven golden roofs. The roofs were built on a system of brackets inserted between the top of a column and a crossbeam, which gives the Potala a unique style. Against the blue sky and white clouds the irregular golden roofs of the Red Palace present a most magnificent scene.

Decorations on Golden Roofs

On the golden roofs are gilded copper vases, columns, and streamers made of silk or yak wool. These decorations standing side by side have a special style. Usually, roofs of important buildings are decorated with gilded columns. For instance, the roofs of the chapels of the Fifth and Thirteenth Dalai Lamas' funerary stupas have the columns in round form or with eight-corners. Other structures have silk and yak wool streamers. The decorations have special meaning in Tibetan Buddhism.

Gilded Vase and Garuda

This picture shows a gilded vase and two garudas on the golden roof of the chapel of the Seventh Dalai Lama's stupa. The vase is called "Vase of Great Treasure." It is in the form of a vase supported by a bell. The vase is a religious object held by a bhikshu or a bodhisattva. In the picture the gilded copper vase is flanked by two garudas on either side. Garuda is a large mythical bird. It wears a beautiful hat and earrings. It has wings on the back and feather patterns on the body. The garudas grasp the chains of the vase with their claws.

Gilded Sea-Turtle Head ◄

The gilded head of the legendary sea-turtle is an important decoration on the golden roofs. It is usually at the front part of a roof ridge. Nevertheless, it also can be seen at the rear part of roof ridge of the chapels that house the Fifth, the Seventh, and the Thirteenth Dalai Lamas' stupas. The head of the legendary turtle has a curled upward nose and horns. It is said that the turtle was evolved from big sea turtles.

Gilded pillar inscribed with Buddhist symbols ◄

There are more than ten gilded copper pillars inscribed with Buddhist symbols around the roofs of the Potala. They are round or octagonal, about 8 feet high. The pillar top is in the form of a flaming "Mani." The pillar is usually inscribed with tassel patterns. It is called Victory Pillar, a symbol of victory, and used for decoration or offering to deities.

Murals under the Eaves

The murals are on the walls on which the "dou-gong" (a system of brackets inserted between the top of a column and a crossbeam) of the golden roofs of the Potala are placed. They are pictures of bodhisattvas, guardian gods, and earth deities.

The Chapel of the Three-Dimensional Mandalas (Lolang Khang)

The chapel is located to the east of the Chapel Celebrating Victory over the Three Worlds. At the center of the chapel are three gilded mandalas built in the time of the Seventh Dalai Lama. The mandala of Guhyasamaja is in the middle. To the right is that of Samvara, and to the left that of Yamantaka. For the three mandalas twelve tablets were made and sent to the Potala by the order of Qing Emperor Qianlong. In addition to the images of the Thirty-five Confessional Buddhas, Sixteen Honored Ones, and ancient Indian monks, there is an image of the Seventh Dalai Lama Kelsang Gyatso. They are either of pure gold or silver. There are also murals about eminent Tibetan monks and monasteries.

Mural Portrait of the Fourth Panchen Lama ◄

On the northern wall of the Mandala Chapel can be seen mural portraits of the successive Panchen Lamas. This picture is only a part of the mural. In the center of the picture is Lokeshvara, with Eleven-headed Avalokiteshvara to his right side. At the left bottom is the Fourth Panchen Lama, who was being ordained to spread Buddhism.

Mural in the Mandala Chapel

The mural is in the Mandala Chapel of the Red Palace. The 38th Tubo Tsenpo Trisong Detsen invited Shantarakshita and Padmasambhava to Tibet, and the three of them built the Samye monastery, the first Buddhist monastery in Tibet. At the same time many Buddhist masters were invited to Tibet from outside to translate Buddhist scriptures and train Tibetan monks. Thus many Tibetans were ordained to be monks, and Buddhism became prosperous in Tibet. The mural depicts how Acharyas and other Buddhist masters practiced Buddhism, worshiped the Buddha, wrote and edited Buddhist works such as "Annotations and Commentaries on Abhisamayalamkara" and "Annotations to the Ashtasahasrika-Prajnaparamita-sutra."

The Chapel Celebrating Victory over the Three Worlds (Sasum Namgyel

In the chapel a painting of Qing Emperor Qianlong hangs over a tablet inscribed with the words "Long, long live the present emperor" in Tibetan, Chinese, Manchurian and Mongolian script. At the southwest side is the statue of Eleven-headed Avalokiteshvara, made with 10,000 ounces of silver as commissioned by the Eighth Dalai Lama. It is surrounded by 2,000 Buddha statues and small pagodas. The chapel hosted many important activities, and is a significant shrine in the Red Palace.

The memorial Tablet to Qing Emperor Kangxi

The tablet is in the shrine on the northern wall of the Chapel Celebrating Victory over the Three Worlds, the highest chapel in the Red Palace. The tablet is near to the tangka portrait of Qing Emperor Qianlong. The tablet is inscribed with characters in Chinese, Tibetan, Manchurian, and Mongolian "A long, long life to the present emperor." The tablet was granted by Yan Xinghu, a grand minister of Qing Emperor Kangxi, to the Seventh Dalai Lama.

► Tangka portrait of Qing Emperor Qianlong

The tangka hangs in the shrine behind the memorial tablet to the Qing Emperor Kangxi. In the tangka Emperor Qianlong wears a monk robe. His right hand makes the gesture of teaching, or turning the wheel of Dharma, and holds a lotus supporting a wisdom knife. His left hand holds a Dharma-wheel and a lotus supporting a Prajnaparamita sutra.

The tangka was granted by the Qing court to the Eighth Dalai Lama for his enthronement ceremony. In the 15th year of the reign of Qianlong (1750), by the Qing court's order, the Kashag, i.e. the former local Tibetan government, was established and handled Tibetan affairs under the leadership of the Amban (Grand minister resident of Tibet) and Dalai Lama. In the 58th year (1793) of the reign of Qianlong, the system of acknowledging the reincarnated Dalai Lama and Panchen Lama by drawing lots from a gold urn was established.

Gilded Copper Mandala of Hevajra

Hevajra is an important supreme yoga tantra deity in Tibetan Buddhism. Hevajra has eight faces, sixteen arms and four legs. Each face has three eyes. He wears a tiara of five skulls. He embraces his consort Nairatma and together they dance on four lesser deities, who symbolize the four demonic forces. Nairatma also wears bone ornaments, holds a curved knife in the right hand, and a skullcup in the left one. They danced on the throne with demons under their feet. The statue of Hevajra, i.e. the main tutelary of the mandala, is in the center of a lotus flower, whose petals are mechanically adjustable.

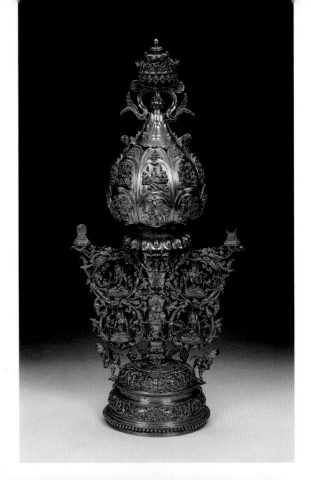

64

The Chapel of Immortal Happiness (Chimey Dedan Kyil)

The main images of this chapel are the gilded copper statues of Amitayus, Vijaya, and White Tara. In niches in the northern wall are the images of Shakyamuni, the Goddess in Leaf-cloth, Sixteen Honored Ones, and the Kadampa Guru. In the niches in the western wall are those of Amitayus, 11-faced Avalokiteshvara, and 35 confessional Buddhas; in the southern and eastern walls can be found a thousand small statues of Amitayus. Besides, there are also a statue of Ekajati, "The Lady of the Single Point," a wrathful female guardian of Dharma, and those of Tsongkhapa and the Three Saviors. On the northern side of the chapel is the throne of the 6th Dalai Lama Tsangyang Gyatso.

The Chapel of Immortal Happiness

This chapel is in the southwest of the 4th floor of the Red Palace. It has 26 square pillars and a skylight window. The chapel is a personal meditation room of the Sixth Dalai Lama Tsangyang Gyatso. On the north side are a throne of the Dalai Lama and a platform for him to preach Buddhism. The shrines along the walls house a thousand gilded copper statues of Amitayus and other Buddhas.

The Three Saviors of the Action Tantra

The statues of the three saviors of the Action Tantra are on the western side of the Chapel of Immortal Happiness, facing east. They wear beautiful crowns and silk robes. The middle one is the statue of Avalokiteshvara. His two hands hold together in front of the chest. To its south is the statue of Manjushri. His right hand holds a sword and his left hand makes a gesture of teaching. To its north is the statue of Vajrapani. His right hand holds a thunderbolt. His left hand makes a gesture of teaching.

Statues of Amitayus

With a look of compassion and dignified appearance, the statue of Amitayus wears a beautiful crown, silk robe, and ear-rings. He is seated on a throne decorated with peacock patterns. His background has patterns of "six sacred beings." Amitayus is also called Amitabha. He is the main object worshipped by the Pure Land sect of exoteric Buddhism, and also regarded as the Buddha of the Pure Land by Tibetan Buddhism.

67

Protectress of the Buddhist Truth

This is a gilded copper statue of Ekajati, a Protectress of Tibetan Buddhism. The statue is on the western side of the Immortal Happiness Chapel. Ekajati wears a tiara of skulls, silk robe and earrings. She has a ferocious appearance, with one hair-knot, one eye, one tooth and one breast. She holds a bleeding heart in her right hand and a wolf in her left hand. She stands on a lotus throne.

Statue of Eminent Buddhist Master ◄

The gilded copper statue of Tsongkhapa is on the western side of the Immortal Happiness Chapel in the Red Palace. Facing east and having a look of compassion, Tsongkhapa wears the robes of a monk and a yellow hat. His two hands are in the gesture of teaching, or turning Dharma-wheel. He is seated on a throne decorated with patterns of birds and animals. The background is of gilded copper patterns of "six sacred beings."

The Chapel for Housing the Thirteenth Dalai Lama's Funerary Stupa

The chapel is located at the western end of the Red Palace, to the west of the Chapel of the Fifth Dalai Lama's Funerary Stupa. Built on the site of formerly monks' dormitories, it was the latest building in the Potala.

It is dedicated to the Thirteenth Dalai Lama's funerary stupa. In this chapel there is an image of the Thirteenth Dalai Lama Thubten Gyatso and various religious objects. The Thirteenth Dalai Lama's life story is shown on the murals on the third floor. Especially, the picture of his monumental visit to Beijing and his audience with Empress Dowager Cixi and Emperor Guangxu in 1908 appears conspicuously on the western wall.

Pearl Mandala

The pearl mandala is in front of the statue of Thirteenth Dalai Lama in the Chapel for housing the Thirteenth Dalai Lama's funerary stupa. The mandala is made with 220,000 pearls, in addition to gold and jewels. The shrine in the center of the mandala has a golden roof. Around the shrine are the figurines of alms-givers, flaming jewels, dharma-wheel, elephant, and horse, etc. The pearl mandala was granted by Empress Dowager Cixi to the Thirteenth Dalai Lama in 1908 (the 34th year of the reign of Emperor Guangxu).

The Statue of the Thirteenth Dalai Lama ▶

The statue is on the western side of the first floor in the Chapel for Housing the Thirteenth Dalai Lama's Funeral Stupa. It faces east, and has a majestic look. The Dalai Lama wears a monk robe, a beautiful silk mantle, and a yellow hat. His right hand makes a gesture of teaching, and the left one holds a dharma-wheel at the chest. He is seated cross-legged on the throne. The Thirteenth Dalai Lama Thubten Gyatso was born in 1876 in Nangxian County of Shannan. At the age of two, he was ordained by the Panchen Lama Tenpai Wangchuk and given the name Thubten Gyatso. At the age of three he was enthroned as the Dalai. At the age of twenty, he took over the government power. At fifty-two he had an audience with Qing Emperor Guangxu in Beijing. In 1933 he died at Norbulingka in Lhasa at the age of fifty-three.

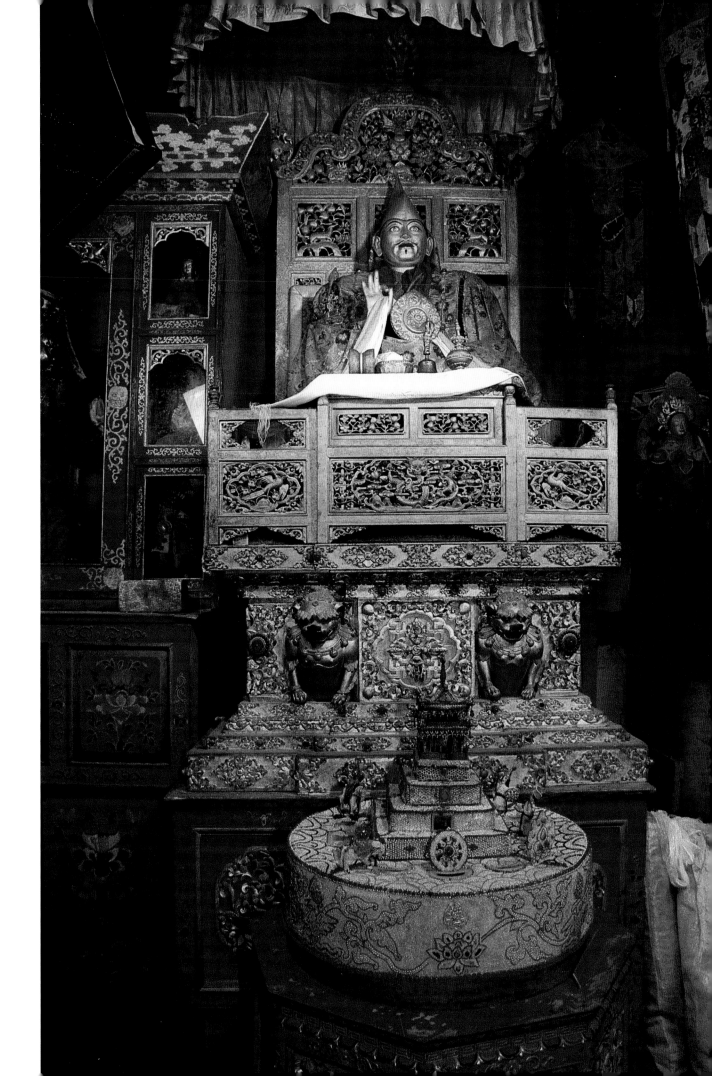

The Funerary Stupa of the Thirteenth Dalai Lama

The stupa is the largest one in the Potala. It is located in the center of the chapel for housing the Thirteenth Dalai Lama's funerary stupa. It looks like a square Bodhi pagoda, facing south; it is 25 feet wide and 42 feet high. It was made of wood coated with gold leafs (for which 1,300 pounds of gold were used) and studded with ten thousand pieces of jade and precious stones. The stupa houses the remains of the Thirteenth Dalai Lama Thubten Gyatso (1876–1933), the sharira of Shakyamuni, a complete set of Kangyur and Tengyur, and many other precious cultural relics.

► The Decorated Top of the Funerary Stupa of the Thirteenth Dalai Lama

The picture shows the decorated top of the Thirteenth Dalai Lama's funerary stupa. One can clearly see the thirteen wheels (yin and yang wheels), streamers, rain-cover, moon, sun, and the top. The stupa reflects the fundamental form of contemporary stupa in Tibet. In Tibet the measurement of stupa construction was based on a Tibetan version of the Indian work on stupa construction entitled Tsugdor Drimey. Since the time when the Potala was extended, Tibet has had a standardized measurement for stupa construction.

Tangka Picture of Amitayus

The tangka hangs in the chapel for housing the Thirteenth Dalai Lama's funerary stupa. The main figure in the tangka is Amitayus. To his right is Avalokiteshvara holding a white lotus, and to his left is Vajrapani holding a thunderbolt. Amitayus holds a bowl with his two hands. He is seated cross-legged on the lotus throne. In Tibetan Buddhism the color of Buddha-body has special meaning. Red means "long life" and "compassion." So Amitayus is in red.

► Shelves for Buddhist scriptures

The shelves along the east and west sides of the chapel for housing the Thirteenth Dalai Lama's funerary stupa contain a complete set of Kangyur.

The Thirteenth Dalai Lama having an Audience with
Qing Emperor Guangxu and Empress Dowager Cixi

The mural is on the west wall of the upper corridor in the chapel for housing the Thirteenth Dalai Lama's funerary stupa in the Red Palace. It depicts the scene of the Thirteenth Dalai Lama having an audience with Emperor Guangxu and Empress Dowager Cixi. In 1908, the Qing government invited the Thirteenth Dalai Lama to Beijing. In Beijing Empress Dowager Cixi and Emperor Guangxu had several interviews with the Dalai Lama.

Mural of Eleven-Headed Avalokiteshvara

The mural is on the southern wall of the upper corridor of the chapel for housing the Thirteenth Dalai Lama's funerary stupa in the Red Palace. The Eleven-Headed Avalokiteshvara holds a lotus in his left hand and a rosary in the right one. His two hands hold together at the chest. The upper part of his body is bare, wearing tassels. He is seated on a lotus throne. His thousand hands with thousand eyes form a halo on his back. Around the image are pictures about the Thirteenth Dalai Lama's achievements.

77

Corridor

The walls of the first, second and third floors of the chapel for keeping the Thirteenth Dalai Lama's funerary stupa in the Red Palace have big colorful murals. On the northern wall of the first floor are pictures of Avalokiteshvara and "Hui-wen" verses (verses that can be read backward or forward and still make sense); on the walls of the second floor are pictures of Guhyasamaja, Vijaya and Yamantaka; and on the third floor are pictures about the Thirteenth Dalai Lama's achievements.

► Corridor

The chapel for keeping the Thirteenth Dalai Lama's funerary stupa in the Red Palace has three floors. The chapel is decorated magnificently and splendidly. The picture shows various decorations in the upper corridor.

The Chapel of Guru (Lama Lhakhang)

The main images include a statue of Tsongkhapa, founder of the Gelukpa order of the Tibetan Buddhism, and those of Tibetan eminent Gurus. The image of Tsongkhapa in the center of the hall is flanked by the statue of the Sixth Dalai Lama on the left and that of the Eighth Dalai Lama on the right. To its south are the statues of the Ninth, Tenth, Eleventh, and Twelfth Dalai Lamas, and to its north are those of the Seventh Dalai Lama and White Tara. The southern and northern shrines are dedicated to more than 1,000 images, including those of Tubo kings and saints, and about 300 Buddhist pagodas. On the shelves on the west wall are placed the Buddhist sutras Kangyur, written in gold ink.

The Statue of the Sixth Dalai Lama

The Sixth Dalai Lama Tsangyang Gyatso (1683--1706) was from Monyul in the south of Tibet. His work "Love Songs" enjoys high reputation in Tibetan literature. He is a romantic intelligent poet. In the 44th year of the reign of Qing Emperor Kangxi (1705), after Depa Sangye Gyatso was murdered by Lhazang Khan, by the emperor's order the Dalai was escorted to Beijing by Mongolian troops. The next year when he reached Qinghai Lake, he died of illness.

The statue of the Sixth Dalai Lama is in the Guru Chapel. He wears a yellow hat and a monk robe. His right hand makes a gesture of teaching, and his left hand holds a dharma-wheel. He is seated cross-legged on the throne. He looks young, handsome, and calm.

The Chapel of the Seventh Dalai Lama's Funerary Stupa

Also called Auspicious Brilliance Stupa Chapel, it is located in the northern corner on the west side of the Red Palace, covering a rather large area. In the center of the hall is the Seventh Dalai Lama's funerary stupa; four seated images of the Seventh Dalai Lama Kelsang Gyatso are placed to the southwest, north, and northeast of the stupa respectively. In front of the stupa are the Harmonious Stupa, Nirvana Stupa, and the Mandala of Yamantaka. A seated image of Maitreya is at the eastern side of the southern wall. In the southern shrine are the statues of White Tara and the eight chief disciples of the Buddha. To the northwest of the stupa are the images of the Past, Present, and Future Buddhas. The Tibetan Tripitaka Tengyur are on the sutra-shelves on the west and north.

Entrance to the Chapel for Housing the Seventh Dalai Lama's Funerary Stupa

The entrance is about 20 feet wide. It is partitioned by four columns into five parts, which have altogether six door-boards. Above the horizontal crossbeam over the entrance are six sets of dou-gong (a system of brackets inserted between the top of a column and a crossbeam), which are bright in color.

The Lokeshvara Chapel (Phakpa Lhakhang)

It is located on the fourth floor of the Red Palace, to the east of the Eighth Dalai Lama's Funerary Stupa, and west of the Seventh Dalai Lama's stupa, and it is directly above the Dharmaraja Cave. The chapel faces south and the central image enshrined in this chapel is a sandalwood statue of Lokeshvara, a tutelary of Songtsen Gampo. The statue is a rare object of the Potala. In a shrine is an image of the Six-headed Yama. There are also other precious Buddhist images and pagodas.

The Board Overhanging the Entrance

A horizontal inscribed board with Qing Emperor Tongzhi's calligraphy "The Amazing Fruits of the Field of Merit" overhangs the entrance of the Lokeshvara Chapel.

► The sandalwood statue of Lokeshvara

The three statues of Lokeshvara are in the shrine on the northern side of the Lokeshvara Chapel in the Red Palace. The middle one is a sandalwood statue of Lokeshvara, made in the reign of Songtsen Gampo in the 7th century. It is said that four statues of Avalokiteshvara were made out of a trunk of a sandalwood tree in Nepal. Two of them were placed in India and Nepal. The third was placed in the Tsukla-khang at Kyirong in Tibet. The fourth one, the statue of Lokeshvara, was placed in the Potala as the yidam (personal tutelary deity) of Songtsen Gampo. At a later time, owing to wars in Tibet, it was moved to other place for a hundred years. In the middle of the 17th century, Tale-gunji, wife of Gushri Khan of the Mongol Hoshot tribe in Qinghai, sent the statue back to the Potala. The statue is considered as the most treasured thing in the Potala. The statue to its left is also a sandalwood statue of Avalokiteshvara, made in the time of the Seventh Dalai Lama, and that to its right is a gilded copper statue of Lokeshvara, made in the time of the Eighth Dalai Lama.

Gilded Dharma-Wheel

The gilded dharma-wheel is on the southern wall in the Lokeshvara Chapel in the Red Palace. In front of it are eight small tablets symbolizing the Eight Auspicious Emblems: auspicious knot, lotus, right-turning conch shell, dharma-wheel, victory banner, vase of great treasure, and two golden fish.

► Thousand-spoke Dharma-wheel

Dharma-wheel is one of the most common Buddhist instruments. Dharma-wheel symbolizes that the teachings of the Buddha are like the wheels of the chariot of a chakravartin, turning around without end. Usually there are two kinds of Dharma-wheel: eight-spoke wheel and thousand-spoke wheel. The dharma-wheel here is a thousand-spoke wheel. The dharma-wheel has five concentric circles, along the rim are patterns of flames, and carved patterns of up-side-down lotus are on its base.

Eight Sugata Stupas

The eight silver stupas are in the shrines of Lokeshvara Chapel in the Red Palace. They are typical Eight Sugata Stupas of Tibetan Buddhism: Enlightenment Stupa, Bodhi Stupa, Auspiciousness Stupa, Miraculous Transformation Stupa, Descent Stupa, Harmonious Stupa, Vijaya Victorious Stupa, and Nirvana Stupa. The eight stupas are in memory of important activities of the Buddha in the world.

Jade Statue of Phakpa

The jade statue of Phakpa is in the shrine of the Lokeshvara Chapel in the Red Palace. Phakpa's full name is Phakpa Lodro Gyaltsen (1235--1280). At the age of ten, he accompanied his uncle Sakya Pandita to Liangzhou in response to the invitation by Prince Godan Khan. When his uncle died he succeeded to his position and became the ruling lama of the Sakya sect. In the Yuan Dynasty he was granted the title of State Preceptor and was in charge of Tibetan political and religious affairs in the Zongzhi (Political) Council. By the Yuan emperor's order he created a new Mongolian script, called Phakpa script. In his old age he went back to the Sakya monastery in Tibet.

Statue of Green Tara

Green Tara, the "Green Saviouress," is one of the patron goddesses of Tibetan Tantra. She is said to be able to save people from eight kinds of disaster, caused by lion, elephant, fire, serpent, thief, prison, floods and non-human-beings. Among the twenty-one Taras, White Tara and Green Tara are most commonly seen. The statue of Green Tara is in a shrine in the Lokeshvara Chapel of the Red Palace. She wears a tiara, and has a look of compassion. Her right hand extended, resting on the knee and making the gesture of fearlessness. In her left hand she holds the stem of a lotus flower. The upper part of her body is bare. With her right leg extending, she sits in royal posture on a throne.

► Statue of Six-Headed Yama

The Six-Headed Yama is called in Tibetan Jampel Shinje Dondrup. The statue is in the shrine on the western side of Lokeshvara Chapel in the Red Palace. The statue is said to have been placed in the Oshangtok Palace (now in Newu Township of Doilung-dechen County of Lhasa, on the other side of the Lhasa River) of Tubo Tsenpo Tritsug Detsen (Ralpachen) during the Tubo period. Afterwards, owing to a fire in the palace, it was moved to the Potala. The Yama has six faces, twelve hands and eighteen eyes. In each of his hands he holds a different religious object. His left leg stretches straight, and his right knee bends. On his back is a hook. The throne on which he stands is obviously not the original one.

Tsongkhapa and His Disciples

The statue is in the shrine on the northern side of the Lokeshvara Chapel in the Red Palace. The gilded copper statues of Tsongkhapa and his disciples constitute a Bodhi tree with Tsongkhapa in its center and his disciples sitting on the branches. Tsongkhapa wears a monk's hat and is seated in the full lotus posture on a lotus throne with a halo behind him. The tree with multiplied branches symbolizes that Tsongkhapa had many disciples. The statue is distinctive in its shape.

► Statue of Eleven-Headed Avalokiteshvara

The statue of eleven-headed Avalokiteshvara is in a shrine on the northern side of the Lokeshvara Chapel in the Red Palace. The Avalokiteshvara has a look of compassion, with downcast eyes. Of the eleven heads in five layers the head of Amitayus on the fifth layer and that of the Wrathful Protector on the fourth layer share a flame-halo. His hands are held to his chest. Wearing streamers, he stands on sun and moon discs supported by a lotus blossom. His thousand hands, each with an eye in the center of the palm, form a big circular halo behind him.

The Chapel of the Eighth Dalai Lama's Funerary Stupa

The chapel is dedicated to the funerary stupa of the Eighth Dalai Lama Jampel Gyatso, with offerings of the Eight Auspicious Symbols and the Seven Royal Treasures. A seated silver image of the Eighth Dalai Lama is in the southwest corner, and on its west and east sides are shelves containing copies of Kangyur written in gold ink. Along the corridors on the upper floor are images of the Fifth Dalai Lama and other figures.

Statue of the Eighth Dalai Lama

The Eighth Dalai Lama Jampel Gyatso (1758–1804) was born at Lharigang in Thobgyal in Tsang. At the age of five, Jampel Gyatso was recognized as the reincarnation of the Seventh Dalai Lama and took his getsul vows from Palden Yeshe, the Sixth Panchen Lama at the Tashilhunpo monastery. He was given the religious name of Losang Tanpel Wangchuk Jampel Gyatso Palzangpo. In 1777 the Sixth Panchen ordained him into full monkhood. At the age of 24, the Dalai took over the power of administration by order of the emperor. Qing Emperor Qianlong granted him a gold album and seal of authority. On the 18th day of the 10th month in the Wood-Cock year of the thirteenth Tibetan calendrical cycle (1804), he died in the Potala at the age of forty-seven.

► Funerary Stupa of the Eighth Dalai Lama

The stupa stands in the center of the chapel for housing the funerary stupa of the Eighth Dalai Lama in the Red Palace. It faces south. It is 31 feet high and 15 feet wide at the base. The stupa is made of wood, coated with gold leaves (of 385 pounds of gold in total). It is in the form of a square Bodhi stupa, which contains the remains of the Eighth Dalai Lama. The stupa is inlaid with pearls, jade and precious stones.

The Chapel of the Ninth Dalai Lama's Funerary Stupa

Known also as The Three Worlds Joy Stupa Chapel, it is located in the east corner at the north side of the fourth floor of the Red Palace, to the west of the Chapel of the Eighth Dalai Lama's Funerary Stupa. It faces south, covering an area of 825 square feet. The chapel is dedicated to the stupa of the Ninth Dalai Lama Lungtok Gyatso. It was built in 1815. In the northwest corner is an image of the Ninth Dalai Lama; and in the northeast corner is a seated image of Tsongkhapa. On the shelves at the east is the Kangyur written in gold ink.

Statue of the Ninth Dalai Lama

The gilded copper statue of the Ninth Dalai Lama is on the northern side of the Ninth Dalai Lama's Stupa Chapel in the Red Palace. The Dalai Lama wears monastic robes and a yellow hat. His right hand makes the gesture of teaching. With childish look, he sits cross-legged on a tall-back throne. The Ninth Dalai Lama Lungtok Gyatso (1805--1815) was born in the present-day Dengke of Sershud County of Garze prefecture in Sichuan province. At the age of three, he was recognized as the reincarnation of the former Dalai Lama. In 1808 he studied with the Seventh Panchen Tenpai Nyima and was ordained and given the name of Losang Tenpai Wangchuk Lungtok Gyatso. At the age of ten he died in the Potala.

The Funerary Stupa of the Ninth Dalai Lama

The stupa is in the center of the Ninth Dalai Lama's Stupa Chapel in the Red Palace. The stupa is made of wood, coated with gold leafs (of 247 pounds of gold). It is in the form of a square Bodhi stupa. It contains the remains of the Ninth Dalai Lama. It is inlaid with all kinds of jewels.

► **Entrance to the Chapel of the Ninth Dalai Lama's Funerary Stupa**

It is about 20 feet wide, and partitioned by four columns into five parts with six door-plants. The lintels above the horizontal beams are beautifully carved.

Murals in the Antechamber

The murals are in the antechamber of the Ninth Dalai Lama's Stupa Chapel in the Red Palace. Two eminent monks of Tibetan Geluk sect are seen in monastic robes and a yellow hat. The one bearing moustache makes a gesture of teaching with his right hand and holds a sutra-book in his left hand. The other holds a thunderbolt (vajra, a scepter-like tantric ritual object) in his right hand and a ritual bell in the left. They are seated cross-legged on their thrones. The officials in beautiful hats and robes hold auspicious offerings, displaying a festival atmosphere.

98

The Kalachakra Chapel (Dukhor Lhakhang)

The chapel is dedicated to a gilded copper mandala of Kalachakra (the Wheel of Time), which was moved from Lhazi to the Potala in the second half of the 17th century. It is surrounded by more than 400 images. In niches in the north wall are images of the Future, Present, and Past Buddhas, Padmasambhava, Pelden Lhamo, the Kalachakra Buddha, and Gurus. Buddhist sutras can also be found here, including the Ashtasahasrika-prajnaparamita-sutra. In niches along the east wall are images of the Eleven-Headed Avalokiteshvara and Vajradhara; and in the southeast is a statue of Padmasambhava.

Part of the Kalachakra Chapel

The Kalachakra Chapel, or Dukhor Lhakhang, is located on the east side of the third floor of the Red Palace. It has eight square pillars. The superb three-dimensional mandala of Kalachakra is in the center of the chapel. In the shrines along the walls are more than 400 images of Buddhas, bodhisattvas and gurus, different in size and material. The picture shows various statues facing south. The wood pagoda in the center is called Dorjeten, or Diamond Throne.

Gilded Three-Dimensional Mandala of Kalachakra

It is in the center of the Kalachakra Chapel of the Red Palace. Each of the four gates on the four sides is 4.5 feet high and 3 feet wide. The mandala was built in accordance with the form of Tantric Mandala. The center is multi-story building, symbolizing the Sumeru, surrounded by pagodas symbolizing the four big continents, eight small continents, and the sun and moon. The mandala was originally kept in the Jolang Phuntsok Ling in Lhaze of Shigatse. In 1680 Depa Sangye Gyatso moved it to the Potala. In 1693 after the Red Palace was completed, the mandala was placed in the Kalachakra Chapel.

► Statue of Kalachakra

Kalachakra, the "Wheel of Time," is a supreme yoga tantra deity. The statue is in the Kalachakra Chapel. Its shape is exquisite. Kalachakra has four faces, twenty-four arms and two legs. He embraces his consort with his two principal arms. She is golden in colour with three heads and eight arms. He stands with one leg straight and the other bending. Underfoot he tramples upon demons. His arms stretching upward, forming a fan-shape, and each hand holds a symbolic tantric implement.

The Chapel of Shakyamuni (Thuwang Lhakhang)

The main figure here is Buddha Shakyamuni. To his left, the main images are Vajrapani, Kshitigarbha, Maitreya and Akashagarbha, and to the right are Avalokiteshvara, Manjushri, Sarvanivara-naviskambini, Samantabhadra, Amitayus, and Dakini. On the south side is a throne of the Seventh Dalai Lama. On a shelf of the east wall is a set of handwritten copies of the Kangyur in gold ink.

Buddhist Scriptures on the Shelves

The Chapel of Shakyamuni, or Thuwang Lhakhang, is in the southeast corner of the third floor of the Red Palace. To its west is the Amitayus Chapel. There are two square pillars in the chapel. Its main statues are those of Shakyamuni and his eight chief disciples. On the south side of the chapel is a statue of the Seventh Dalai Lama. The picture shows the scene inside the chapel. On the shelves are Buddhist scriptures Kangyur in gold ink.

▶ **Statue of Shakyamuni**

The gilded silver statue of Shakyamuni is in the shrine on the west wall. To the south of the shrine are the statues of Avalokiteshvara, Manjushri, Sarvanivara-naviskambini, and Samantabhadra; and to the north are those of Vajrapani, Kshitigarbha, Maitreya, and Akashagarbha. Besides, in the shrines at the south side are Dakini, Amitayus, and "Tenthar-Lingma."

102

The Chapel of Amitayus (Tsepagme Lhakhang)

Located in the south of the third floor, it can be reached from the Secretary Office in the west and the Shakyamuni Chapel in the east. It faces south and has four square pillars. Nine statues of Amitayus dominated this chapel, with a gilded copper one in the center. Two gilded images of Green Tara and White Tara are also presented, one on the west and the other on the east. Besides, there are many other images and pagodas. In the south is a throne of the Eighth Dalai Lama.

Statue of Amitabha

This gilded copper statue is the main image in the Chapel of Amitabha. It is on the northern side of the chapel, facing south. Amitabha wears a five-petal crown. He sits cross-legged on the throne. The Sanskrit Amitabha literally means "The one of Infinite Life." Amitabha is the center of the worship of the Pure Land school of Chinese Buddhism. Amitabha is considered as ruler of the western paradise Sukhavati.

The Chapel of Shakyamuni of Virtues (Shakya Lhakhang)

The chapel is in the southwest corner of the third floor of the Red Palace. The central figure in the chapel is the statue of Shakyamuni, the founder of Buddhism. It is among his other enshrined sandalwood images, presenting his life-stories, and those of the sixteen arhats. In the south at the west pillar is a gilded copper statue of the Fifth Dalai Lama, and at the east pillar is that of the Seventh Dalai Lama. The chapel also houses about a hundred Buddha statues made of various materials.

Sandalwood Statue of Shakyamuni

The main statue of the chapel is a medicated clay sculpture of Shakyamuni. But this one is of sandalwood.

The Dharmaraja Cave (Chogyel Drupug)

Located on the top of the Red Hill, this cell, built in the 7th century, is one of the oldest rooms in the Potala. It faces south, covering an area of 340 square feet. Songtsen Gampo, known as Dharmaraja, is said to have used this cell as his meditation chamber. The cell has the images of Songtsen Gampo, Princess Wencheng, Princess Trisun, Gar Tongtsan, and Tonmi Sambhota, in addition to early rare murals and color clay sculptures.

Statue of Songtsen Gampo

The statue is on the northern side of the Dharmaraja Cave of the Red Palace. Made in the mid-17th century, the statue is a painted clay sculpture. Songtsen Gampo wears a cloth turban and silk robes. He was the 33rd Tubo Tsenpo. He moved the capital city to Rasa (the present-day Lhasa) and unified the Qinghai-Tibetan plateau. During his reign the Tibetan written language was created, Buddhist scriptures were translated into Tibetan, and Six Main Laws were made. He married Nepalese Princess Trisun and Tang Princess Wencheng, and built the Jokhang and Ramoche temples.

Statue of Ajita Arhat

Ajita is one of the sixteen "worthy ones." He lives with a thousand arhats in the snow-capped Mount Kailas. In Buddhist canons Shakyamuni asked the sixteen "worthy ones" to live as Buddhist saints in sixteen different places. The sixteen "worthy ones" are also called sixteen arhats. The earliest statues of the sixteen arhats in Tibet were made in the 10th century and placed in the Tongta Yerpa temple of Lhasa. They are in the style of the then Tang sculpture. So, till now the arhats still wear Tang clothes with loose sleeves, though their images are Indian in style in later development.

Statue of Princess Wencheng

The statue is on the northern side of the Dharma-raja Cave of the Red Palace. It was made in the mid-17th century. The statue is a painted clay sculpture. Her face displays a feeling of piousness. She is decorous and elegant in appearance. In 641, Tang Emperor Taizong married Princess Wencheng, a daughter from the royal family, to Tubo Tsenpo Songtsen Gampo. She brought to Tibet a statue of Shakyamuni, jewels, Buddhist scriptures, medical books, seeds, cotton and silk, making great contributions to the development of Tubo economy and culture.

Statue of Princess Trisun (Bhrkuti)

The statue is on the northern side of the Dharma-raja Cave of the Red Palace. It was made in the mid-17 century. The statue is a painted clay sculpture. Prince Trisun has high nose and deep-set eyes. Her face displays a feeling of piousness. Her palms are he together at the chest. Her father Amshuvarman, Nepalese king, married her to Songtsen Gampo in 63

She brought to Tibet a statue of Shakyamuni, Mahayana scriptures, handicrafts, and craftsmen. With Princess Wencheng's help, she built the Jokhang Temple. She made positive contributions to Tubo cultural development.

Statue of Tonmi Sambhota

The statue is on the western side of the Dharma-raja Cave of the Red Palace. It was made in the mid-17th century. The statue is a painted clay sculpture. He is refined in appearance, and wears silk clothes. Tonmi Sambhota was a minister of Songtsen Gampo. He was sent to study Sanskrit and Buddhism in India. He created a system of Tibetan written language system by using the vowels and consonants of Sanskrit and Tibetan tones.

Statue of Gar Tongtsan

The statue is on the eastern side of the Dharma-raja Cave of the Red Palace. It faces towards north to Princess Wencheng and Princess Trisun. It was made before the mid-17th century. The statue is a painted clay sculpture. He wears silk robes. He was a minister of Songtsen Gampo. He helped the Tsenpo to make a law system, and acted as go-between for the Tsenpo to marry his Nepalese and Chinese wives. A Tang painter named Yan Liben made a picture of Tang Emperor Taizong granting an interview to Gar Tongtsan as a Tubo envoy who came to ask the hand of Princess Wencheng for Songtsen Gampo. He helped the Tubo king to administrate Tibet for about half a century.

Statue of Gungri Gungtsan

The statue is in the northwest corner of the Dharma-raja Cave of the Red Palace. It was made in mid-17th century. The statue is a painted clay sculpture. Gungri Gungtsan wears cloth turban. He was son of Songtsen Gampo, but he died young without ascending to the throne. His son Mangsong Mangtsan succeeded Songtsen Gampo as the Tubo king in 650.

► **A Mural Made in the Tubo Period**

The mural is in the Dharma-raja Cave; it was a mural made in the 7th century. It was found on the east and south walls when the Cave was in repair in 1989-1994. The mural is about a Tubo minister. It was painted with delicate skills.

110

The Chapel of Samantabhadra (Kunzang Lhakhang)

The chapel is located in the center of the northern side on the third floor of the Red Palace. The main figure is a gilded copper statue of Shakyamuni, flanked by the images of Avalokiteshvara, the Fifth Dalai Lama, Vajrakumara, Yamantaka, Vajrapani, Padmasambhava, Maitreya, Hayagriva, and the eight chief disciples of the Buddha. Buddha images and pagodas donated by Buddhist followers in 1994 are also kept in the chapel.

Statue of Shakyamuni

This is the image on the north wall in the Dharma-raja Cave. It is a gilded copper statue of Shakyamuni.

Statue of Vajradhara

The statue is in the Chapel of the Example of Samantabhadra. His body is dark-blue. With angry look and upward hair he wears a tiger-skin around his waist, precious tassels, and streamers. He holds a thunderbolt in his right hand and a vajra-bell in the left, displaying the wrathful aspect of the bodhisattva of Vajra Tantra division when subduing demons. Vajradhara is the tantric manifestation of Shakyamuni Buddha and the Secret Lord of Tantra.

The Chapel of Brass Statues (Lima Lhakhang)

Located at the east end of the third floor of the Red Palace, the chapel consists of two communicable side-by-side apartments. The chapel houses more than 3,000 statues of Shakyamuni and other Buddhist saints, of which 1,700 are cast in brass, and the other 1,200 are of other materials. The main figure is a brass statue of Shakyamuni. In addition, the chapel has 287 Buddhist pagodas, of which 280 are of brass. About 100 statues are marked with Chinese characters "Made in Great Ming Xuande period" or "Made in Great Ming Yongle period." The rest were made in India, Nepal, Mongolia, and Tibet.

Statue of Guru ◄

The Guru is the Nirmanakaya of Padmasambhava. He wears Tibetan Buddhist scholar's hat and a monastic robe. On the hat are symbols of sun and moon, representing the brilliant source, convenience to vow-giving, and complete wisdom. His right hand holds a phurba, and the left hand makes a gesture of holding a skullcup. He is seated on a lotus throne with one leg stretching and the other one bending. His two consorts stand on his either side. His background is made of tree-branch patterns, with an image of Amitabha at the upper center, flanked by eight small images representing the eight title-names of Padmasambhava: Sakya Senge, Padmakara, Nyima Ozer, Senge Dradrok, Guru Dorje Drolo, Padma Vajra, Padma Gyalpo and Guru Loden Chokse.

Statue of Tsongkhapa

Tsongkhapa Losang Drakpa (1357–1419) was a great Tibetan Buddhist philosopher and the founder of Tibetan Buddhist Geluk Sect, which has had the greatest influences in Tibet. At the age of sixteen, he studied very well the exoteric and esoteric Buddhism. At twenty-five, he was ordained and became a bhikshu. At thirty-eight, he was engaged in the reform of Tibetan Buddhism, writing Buddhist works and preaching Buddhism. Thus the Geluk sect, which emerged later than the other sects of Tibetan Buddhism, occupied eminent position in Tibetan Buddhism. The statue of Tsongkhapa is in the Bronze Chapel of the Red Palace. With the exaggerated size of his head his monastic hat is striking. He wears the robes of a monk. The statue was excellently made.

Kadam Stupa

The Kadam stupa is in the Bronze Chapel of the Red Palace. The Potala has several hundred stupas of different weight, shape and material. The biggest one is 42.54 feet (12.97meters) high, and the smallest less than 0.03 feet (0.01meter) high. In shape, most fall into the category of the Eight-Sugata stupas, with a small number of Kadam stupas and of other variations. The material for them includes gold, silver, gold-plated, silver-plated, gilded, alloy, copper, wood, stone, clay, crystal, jade, etc. Most Kadam stupas are of alloy. The stupa is like the Indian Buddhist stupa in the form of a bell.

Wooden Stupa

The wooden stupa is in the Bronze Chapel of the Red Palace. The Mahabodhi Stupa (Tibetan: Dorjeten, or Diamond Throne) is at Bodh Gaya, India, where Shakyamuni was enlightened. Therefore, Tibetan Buddhist followers made many small-sized Mahabodhi stupas and regarded them as objects of worship. They were usually made of metal or wood.

The Corridors of Murals on the Second Floor of the Red Palace

The corridors on the second floor of the Red Palace are flanked with frescoed walls. The murals make up a great part of the murals in the Potala and the corridors can be rated as an art gallery. On the western wall are the images of the Fifth Dalai Lama, Desi Sangye Gyatso, Dalai Khan, and Tibetan officials. On the northern wall from west to east are pictures of the "Religious activities at the Ganden Monastery," "Conversion of the Tsedor Monastery into Gelukpa Order," "Death of Desi Trinley Gyatso," "Construction of a pagoda at the Reting Monastery," "Buddhist activities at the Drepung Monastery" and the "Monasteries in other parts of Tibet." On the eastern wall from north to south are pictures of "The omens for the Fifth Dalai Lama's funerary stupa to be placed in the Potala," "Buddhist activities for the construction of the Fifth Dalai Lama's funerary stupa," and "The extension project of the Potala." On the southern wall from east to west are pictures of "The construction of gilded roof of the Red Palace," "Buddhist Activities," "Prayer meeting at the Jokhang Temple," "Displaying the picture of the Buddha," "Buddhist activities in Shannan," and "Prayer meeting and the offerings to the Buddha." On the north side of the western wall is a series of pictures about "Buddhist activities for the completion of the construction of the Potala." These pictures display the whole process of the construction of the Potala, the inauguration ceremony for the Red Palace, and the prayer meeting held at the Ramoche Temple the following year.

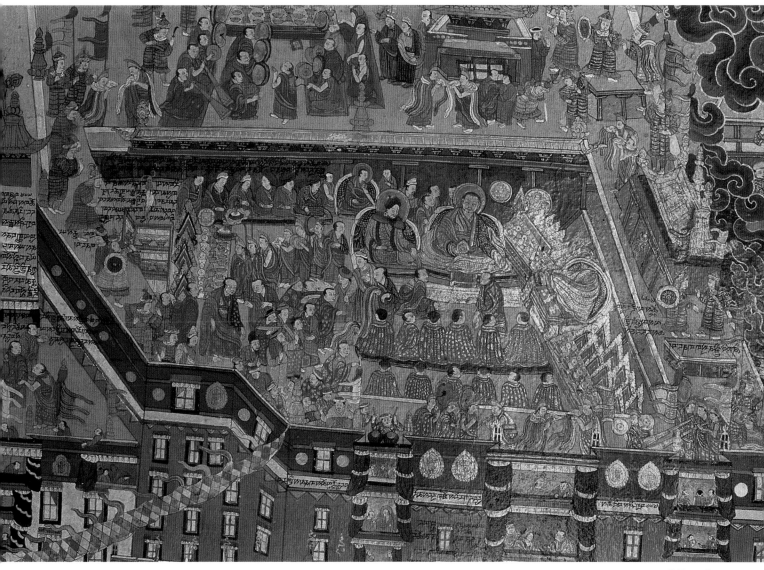

Mural—Burnt Offering ◄

The mural is on the southern wall of the corridor of the second floor in the Red Palace. In 1682, the Fifth Dalai Lama died. Because of political and religious reasons, Depa Sangye Gyatso had not reported the Dalai Lama's death to the Qing Court for more than ten years. In 1690, Sangye Gyatso sponsored the construction of the Fifth Dalai Lama's funerary stupa and the chapel for housing it. For this, the Red Palace was enlarged. In 1693, on the 20th day of the fourth month of the Tibetan calendar, a grand ceremony was held for celebrating the completion of the reconstruction of the Red Palace. The mural depicts the grand ceremonies including burnt offering, etc.

Mural

The mural is on the south wall of the corridor of the second floor in the Red Palace. The mural depicts the grand ceremony held for celebrating the completion of reconstruction of the Red Palace.

► Mural of a Big Religious Assembly

The mural is on the south wall of corridor of the second floor in the Red Palace. In 1694, a year after the enlargement of the Red Palace, a big religious assembly was held in commemoration of the Fifth Dalai Lama. After that, whenever a Dalai Lama died the day for the religious assembly would be one day longer than the last one. The mural presents the magnificent scene of the Buddhist rituals. Two tangka pictures hang on the southern wall of the Potala for showing the Buddha's image. Monks and lay people inside and outside the Potala are dancing and singing, and earnestly praying to the Buddha.

Mural

The mural is on the southern wall of the corridor on the second floor of the Red Palace. The mural depicts the grand ceremony held for celebrating the completion of reconstruction of the Red Palace. There is archery from horseback, and wrestling.

Mural

The mural is on the west wall of the corridor of the second floor of the Red Palace. The mural depicts a grand ceremony held for celebrating the completion of the Red Palace. In the East Courtyard monks are giving gifts to devout believers. Buddhist followers are performing folk dances, including lion dance, tiger dance, and yak dance.

The West Audience Hall (Sishi Phuntsok Hall)

With an area of over 860 square yards and 44 pillars, it is the largest hall in the Potala. On the west side is the throne of the Fifth Dalai Lama, over which is the panel presented by Qing Emperor Qianlong with its Chinese characters written in gold, which read: "The Holy Spot of the Emerging Lotus." Murals cover all the walls. Around the corridors on the second floor, on the northern side is a picture of the Fifth Dalai Lama, on the western a picture of Shakyamuni, on the eastern a picture of Tsongkhapa and his two chief disciples. On the western wall around the first-floor hall are pictures of the Buddha's stories and the picture of the First Dalai Lama. Those on the northern wall are pictures of the Eleven-Headed Avalokiteshvara and the Fifth Dalai Lama's achievements. On the eastern wall are the picture of the Fifth Dalai Lama's audience with the Qing Emperor Shunzhi in Beijing in 1652, which is important as an artistic masterpiece and a historical record, and pictures of Songtsen Gampo and Trisong Detsen. On the southern wall were painted the pictures of Drom Tonpa, the founder of the Kadam order, Gyelwa Jungne, Nyang Nyima Ozer, and the Fifth Dalai Lama's achievements. The exposed beams of the hall are decorated with hollowed-out images of Buddha or patterns of animals and other objects.

The West Audience Hall

The West Audience Hall is the memorial hall of the Fifth Dalai Lama's funerary stupa, and also a place where the ceremonies for successive Dalai Lamas' enthronement and assumption of office were held. On the west side of the hall is the throne of the Dalai Lama. The murals in this hall consist mainly of the stories about the Fifth Dalai Lama during his lifetime and events of his reign.

Mural Showing the Fifth Dalai Lama Having an Audience with Qing Emperor Shunzhi

The mural, 10.50 feet high, is on the east side of the West Audience Hall. In 1652, the Fifth Dalai Lama Ngawang Losang Gyatso and his party left Ganden Potrang of Drepung Monastery in Lhasa for Beijing. Qing Emperor Shunzhi gave them a warm welcome. The mural depicts the important historical event.

Horizontal Board Bearing Qing Emperor Qianlong's Calligraphy, and the Throne of the Dalai Lama ►

The West Audience Hall (Sishi Phuntsok Hall) is the largest hall in the Red Palace. The Dalai Lama's throne here does not face south as it usually does in other halls. The throne in this hall is in front of the western wall, because the Chapel for Housing the Fifth Dalai Lama's Funerary Stupa is located to its west side. Over the throne of the Dalai Lama hangs a horizontal board bearing Qing Emperor Qianlong's calligraphy "Holy Spot of the Emerging Lotus."

The Chapel of the Stages on the Path to Enlightenment (Lamrim Lhakhang)

The chapel has as its main figure a gilded silver statue of Tsongkhapa, founder of the Gelukpa order, with statues of the Fifth Dalai Lama and Songtsen Gampo at the left and right pillars. Two Enlightenment Stupas are on both sides. In the niches along the northern wall are the masters of the "extensive" lineage and along the southern wall are the masters of the "profound" lineage. There is also a tangka of Tara.

The Chapel of the Stages on the Path to Enlightenment

The Chapel of the Stages on the Path to Enlightenment, or Lamrim Lhakhang, is on the east side of the first floor in the Red Palace. It faces south and covers an area of 114 square yards. The picture shows a part of it from north to south. In the center of the hall is a gilded silver statue of Tsongkhapa, flanked by the statue of Songtsen Gampo and that of the Fifth Dalai Lama.

Statue of Tsongkhapa

The gilded silver statue of Tsongkhapa is in the center of the Chapel of the Stages on the Path to Enlightenment. It faces west and is the main image of the chapel. Tsongkhapa (1357–1419) was the founder of the Geluk sect of Tibetan Buddhism. At the age of three, he was ordained, and at the age of seven, he took his getsul vows. After thirty-seven, he engaged in the reformation of Tibetan Buddhism. He was a master of the Exoteric and Esoteric Tibetan Buddhism and author of many works. His two most celebrated works are *The Great Exposition of the Stages on the Path to Enlightenment* and *The Great Exposition of Tantra*. In 1409 he was in charge of the construction of Ganden Monastery, the first monastery of Geluk sect. Tsongkhapa had many disciples, of whom the eminent are Gyeltsab Je (the first Tripa of Ganden Monastery), Khedrup Je (the first Panchen Lama), and Gendun Drup (the first Dalai Lama).

The Knowledge Holders' Chapel (Rigzin Lhakhang)

A silver statue of Padmasambhava, founder of Tibetan Buddhist Nyingmapa order, is in the center of the chapel. He is flanked by his Tibetan consort Yeshe Tsogyel and Bengalese consort Mandarava. On the eastern side are eight gilded copper statues of the Eight Knowledge Holders. On the western side are eight statues of his various manifestations, i.e. Guru Vajradhara (Bearer of the Vajra), Guru Loden Chokse (Intelligent Seeker of the highest Truth), Guru Nyima Ozer (Ray of the Sun), Senge Dradrok (Lion's Roar), Padmasambhava, Guru Padma Gyalpo (Lotus King), Guru Shakya Senge (Lion of the Shakyas), and Guru Dorje Drolo. Besides, these are supplemented by images of Three Saviors and eight silver pagodas dedicated to Sugata.

Wood Engraving on the Seats of the Statues

The four wood sculptures are in the shrines facing north in the center of the Knowledge-holders' Chapel. Peacock, lion, elephant, horse, Garuda and mighty man are the "six sacred beings." The four sculptures of horse, elephant, peacock and Garuda are considered as guardians of living beings and symbols of happiness in Tibetan Buddhism.

The Chapel of the Fifth Dalai Lama's Funerary Stupa (Sedong Khang)

Built in 1690, the chapel is a 3-storied hall building with 16 pillars. The Fifth Dalai Lama's stupa is in the center. To its right side is the Tenth Dalai Lama's stupa, gilded with gold foils, and to its left is the stupa of the Twelfth Dalai Lama. Along the walls are eight kinds of Tathagata Stupas made of silver: Descent Stupa, Harmonious Stupa, Nirvana Stupa, and Bodhi Stupa on the northern side; and Auspicious Stupa, Miraculous Stupa, Vijaya Victorious Stupa and Enlightenment Stupa on the southern side.

The Funerary Stupa of the Fifth Dalai Lama

The stupa, facing east, is in the center of the Chapel of the Fifth Dalai Lama's Funerary Stupa in the Red Palace; it is in the form of a Bodhi stupa. It is of wood coated with gold leaves (for which 8,223 pounds of gild were used), and studded with 15,000 pieces of jewels. It is 41 feet high and 25 feet wide at the base. It houses the remains of the Fifth Dalai Lama Ngawang Losang Gyatso (1617-1682), an edict of Songtsen Gampo, a Buddhist scripture written on palm-leaves entitled *Annotations and Commentaries on Kalachakra*, the first handwritten copy of *Book of Teachings by Five Kinds of Teachers*, and other rare cultural relics.

Statue of Padmasambhava ◄

The statue is in the center of the Knowledge Holders' Chapel in the Red Palace. Facing north, it is 6.5 feet high and 5.25 feet wide. Padmasambhava holds a phurba (a ritual dagger) in his right hand and a skullcup in the left. He sits cross-legged in a royal position on a lotus throne. He came from Orgyen in the northwest of India. He mastered the exoterism and esoterism and founded a school of his own. In 760, he was invited by Tubo Tsenpo Trisong Detsen to Tibet, where he propagated Vajrayana Tantra and built Samye Monastery, the first Buddhist monastery in Tibet. He was worshipped as the founder of Tibetan Buddhist Tantra and the founder of the Nyingma sect.

The Stupa of the Tenth Dalai Lama

The stupa, facing east, is to the north of the Fifth Dalai Lama's stupa. It is round, in the form of a Vijaya stupa. It was made of wood and coated with gold-leaves (for which 243 pounds of gold were used), and studded with several thousand pieces of jewels. It is 23 feet high. It contains the remains of the Tenth Dalai Lama Tsultrim Gyatso (1816-1837) and Buddhist scriptures and cultural relics.

► The Stupa of the Twelfth Dalai Lama

The stupa, facing east, is to the south of the Fifth Dalai Lama's stupa. It is round, in the form of a Vijaya stupa. It is made of wood and coated with gold-leaves, and studded with jewels. At 24 feet high, it contains the remains of the Twelfth Dalai Lama Trinley Gyatso (1858-1875) and Buddhist scriptures and cultural relics.

The Chapel of the Holy Born (Trungrab Lhakhang)

In the center of the chapel are a gold statue of Shakyamuni and a silver one of the Fifth Dalai Lama. To their right are the statues of the First through the Fourth Dalai Lamas, and to their left Eight Medicine Buddhas. At the western wall are the gilded stupa and a seated image of the Eleventh Dalai Lama Khedrup Gyatso. On the shelves against the eastern and northern walls are the Tengyur.

Statue of the Eleventh Dalai Lama

The statue is on the west side of the Chapel of the Holy Born in the Red Palace. The Eleventh Dalai Lama Khedrup Gyatso (1838-1855) was born in a rich family near Kangding County of Sichuan. At the age of three, he was selected as one of the candidates for the reincarnation of the Tenth Dalai Lama. At the age of four, he was finally recognized as the reincarnation of the Tenth Dalai Lama after he and the other three candidates had drawn lots from the Golden Urn in the Potala. When he was eight years old, he was ordained by the Seventh Panchen Lama Tenpai Nyima. At the age of seventeen, he assumed the power of administration, but less than one year later he died in the Potala.

► Shakyamuni and the Fifth Dalai Lama

The two statues are in the center of the Chapel of the Holy Born. Facing south, the two images sit cross-legged each on a throne. The left one is the statue of Shakyamuni, which is made of pure gold (116 pounds of gold were used). The statue was made after the example of the life-size image of Shakyamuni at the age of twelve, which is in the Jokhang Temple. The right one is the statue of the Fifth Dalai Lama, which is made of pure silver (86 pounds of silver were used). With looks of resolution, he wears monastic robes and a yellow hat. His right hand makes a gesture of teaching, and his left hand holds a dharma-wheel.

The Stupa of the Eleventh Dalai Lama

The stupa is on the west side of the Holy Born Chapel. Facing south, it is 22.6 feet high and 11.6 feet wide at the base. It is square in the form of a Bodhi stupa. It is made of wood and coated with gold leaves, and studded with thousand pieces of diamond, conch shell and jewels. The stupa contains the remains of the Eleventh Dalai Lama (1838-1855), Buddhist scriptures and cultural relics. In the niche at the entrance of the stupa is an image of Songtsen Gampo.

Statue of the First Dalai Lama Gendun Drupa

The statue is the fourth one to the east of the gilded silver statue of the Fifth Dalai Lama, which is in the center of the Holy Born Chapel in the Red Palace. The First Dalai Lama Gendun Drupa (1391-1474) was born in Sakya County of Tibet. His original name was Padma Dorje. At the age of fifty-seven, he was in charge of the construction of Tashilhunpo monastery at Shigatse. Afterwards, he was the abbot of Tashilhunpo monastery for 26 years. He was posthumously recognized as the First Dalai Lama.

Statue of the Second Dalai Lama Gendun Gyatso

The statue is the fifth one to the east of the gilded silver statue of the Fifth Dalai Lama, which is in the center of the Holy Born Chapel in the Red Palace. The Second Dalai Lama Gendun Gyatso (1475-1542) was a native of Shatongmon County in Tsang. His original name is Sengge Pal. At the age of seven he was identified as the reincarnation of the First Dalai Lama. At the age of ten he took getsul vows from Panchen Lama Longri Gyatso and was given the name of Gendun Gyatso. He took the position of abbot of the Tashilhunpo, Drepung, and Sera monasteries successively.

Statue of the Third Dalai Lama Sonam Gyatso

The statue is the sixth one to the east of the gilded silver statue of the Fifth Dalai Lama, which is in the center of the Holy Born Chapel in the Red Palace. The Third Dalai Lama Sonam Gyatso (1543-1588) was a native of Tohlung Dechen in Tibet. Invited by Altan Khan, he went to Qinghai in 1577. Altan Khan granted him the title of the "Dalai Lama." He went with Altan Khan to Mongolia, spreading Buddhism. He died in Mongolia.

Statue of the Fourth Dalai Lama Yonten Gyatso

The statue is the seventh one to the east of the gilded silver statue of the Fifth Dalai Lama, which is in the center of the Holy Born Chapel in the Red Palace. The Fourth Dalai Lama Yonten Gyatso (1589-1616) was a Mongolian. His father was the grandson of Altan Khan. When he was identified as the reincarnation of the Third Dalai Lama he was given the religious name of Yonten Gyatso. At the age of twenty-six he was ordained by the Fourth Panchen Lama. He took the position of abbot of the Sera and Drepung monasteries successively.

Cultural Relics Collected in the Potala

The Potala has an enormous collection of cultural relics, including Buddhist pagodas, statues, murals, tangka paintings, and scriptures. There preserved are also such relics as the emperors' edicts, the gold, silver, and jade appointment certificates and seals of authority, which the Ming and Qing emperors granted to the successive Dalai Lamas. There is also an immense treasure of golden, silver, jade, and porcelain utensils, and precious palm-leaf sutras. They are of high economical and historical value.

Jade Album Inscribed with the Edict of Qing Emperor Qianlong Conferring the Recognition of the Eighth Dalai Lama

This jade album inscribed with words in the Tibetan, Chinese, Manchurian, and Mongolian scripts. It has eight plates; each plate is 9 inches long, 4 inches wide and 0.2 inch thick, and 6 pounds in weight. The carved lines of the words and dragon-and-cloud patterns are filled with gold. The jade album is now collected in the Tibetan Museum.

Gold Album Inscribed with the Edict of Qing Emperor Daoguang Conferring the Recognition of the Eleventh Dalai Lama

The gold album, which was granted to the Eleventh Dalai Lama Khedrup Gyatso by Qing Emperor Daoguang, bears an inscription in Tibetan, Chinese, Manchurian, and Mongolian. It has 13 plates; each is 9 inches long, 4 inches wide and 0.2 inch thick. The album is now kept in the Tibetan Museum.

The Gold Seal and Its Inscription Issued to the Dalai Lama by the Qing Emperor Shunzhi

The gold seal is 4 inches high, 4.5 inches long and 18.34 pounds in weight. In 1652 the Fifth Dalai Lama was invited by the emperor to the capital city of Beijing for an audience. The next year when the Dalai Lama was on the way back to Tibet, he received a title-conferring gold-gilt album and a gold seal of authority from the emperor. The gold seal bore in Manchurian, Chinese, and Tibetan the inscription "The Seal of the Dalai Lama, Buddha of Great Compassion in the West, Leader of the Buddhist Faith beneath the Sky, Holder of the Vajra." The gold seal of authority granted to the Seventh Dalai Lama by the emperor Yongzheng in the second year of Yongzheng reign bore an inscription in Chinese, Tibetan, Manchurian and Mongolian.

Religious Dance Masks

Tibetan religious dance has various masks and they vary from monastery to monastery. There are masks of Dharmaraja and his consort, guardian-king, Hayagriva, Yamantaka, Pelden Lhamo, Yama, ghost, Earth-deity, hunter, child, deity, monk, Shitavana Lord, deer, lion, yak and horse, etc. Here are two masks from a complete collection of masks collected in the Potala.

Religious Dance Costume

Religious dance has a long history in Tibetan Buddhism. In the period of Tubo Tsenpo Trisong Detsen, Samye Monastery, the first Buddhist monastery in Shannan of Tibet was built. Padmasambhava held an inauguration ceremony for it by way of performing religious dance on the basis of Tantric Vajra-dance. In the "Latter prosperity of Buddhism," Rinchen Sampo, a Tibetan Buddhist master in Toling monastery, developed the Tantric Vajra-dance. Since then the monasteries of all Tibetan Buddhist sects have preserved the dance for spreading Buddhism. On the 29th day of the 12th month of every year by Tibetan calendar, the monks of Namgyel Dratsang in the Potala would perform the dance, wearing religious dance costumes and masks, in the East Courtyard.

The Kangyur Sutra in Tibetan, Chinese, Manchurian and Mongolian

This set of the Kangyur of Tripitaka is collected in the Potala. It was written with mineral paints, gold, silver, copper, iron, turquoise, red coral and pearls. The Tripitaka of Tibetan Buddhism includes Kangyur (the Buddha's words) and Tengyur (the Buddha's disciples' commentaries on the Buddha's words). There are various editions of Tengyur of Tibetan Tripitaka.

Pattra-Leaf Scripture

Before papermaking technique was introduced to India, the Indians used pattra leaves for writing. Pattra-leaf scripture was written on pattra-leaves. As tree leaves are difficult to preserve, the pattra-leave scriptures are very precious. Owing to the dry weather and thin air on the Tibetan plateau, many early pattra-leaf scriptures have been preserved till now. This scripture is in Sanskrit.

Larger Prajnaparamita-sutra

The Prajnaparamita sutras are a group of sutras about prajna
(wisdom) paramita, or the complete wisdom. They consist of
Larger Prajnaparamita-sutra, Middle Prajnaparamita-sutra, and
Small Prajnaparamita-sutra. The Larger Prajnaparamita-sutra,
Middle Prajnaparamita-sutra, and Small Prajnaparamita-sutra
have a hundred thousand verses, twenty thousand verses and
eight thousand verses respectively. The sutra here is the second
fascicle of the Larger Prajnaparamita-sutra.

► Phurba

Phurba is a tantric ritual dagger, which is an embodiment
of Buddha-activities. The ritual implement has a triangular
blade. The upper handle has a decoration of a head with
three wrathful faces and a handle-top. The shaft-base for
the phurba is triangular. The upper handle and the base are
gilded and engraved with patterns. The phurba is used for
subduing demons.

A Tea Set

This is a high-quality tea set for high-ranking people to drink buttered tea. The saucer and cover are of gilded silver. The saucer looks like a lotus in full blossom. The cover is terraced in form, and its top inlaid with a round red coral. The saucer and cover are decorated with engraved patterns of good augury.

Incense burners

This pair of gilded silver incense burners are collected in the Potala; they are 1.5 feet high. The incense burner consists of the body, cover and chain-handle. The body has a round mouth and a bulged belly. On the belly in the middle part are engraved patterns of the Chinese character Xi, which means happiness, and in the upper part are S-shaped patterns. The burner's foot has lotus patterns. The handle is like a dragon with an arched back. The cover is terraced in form, and its knob is like a lotus-bud. The cover is hollowed out, so that the fragrance can go out. The cover has patterns of dragon, flower and grass. Incense burners of this kind are usually used at grand religious and festival ceremonies, and specially trained personnel were assigned to take charge of them.

Statue of Shakyamuni

Shakyamuni is the founder of Buddhism. His name was Siddhartha Gautama. He was son of Shuddhodana, king of an ancient Indian kingdom Kapilavastu. At the age of twenty-nine, he left home to find the way to enlightenment. At the age of thirty-five, he attained enlightenment and became the Buddha. He died at Kusinara at the age of eighty. He was respectfully called the "Buddha." The Buddha was of complete enlightenment, and also a savior of all living beings. In Tibetan Buddhism the image of Shakyamuni was traditionally made in two forms: one is of Tathagata image and the other is of Bodhisattva image. The image here is of the second form.